How to Live
Green, Cheap, and Happy

How to Live
Green, Cheap, and Happy
Save Money! Save the Planet!

Randi Hacker

STACKPOLE
BOOKS

Published by
STACKPOLE BOOKS
5067 Ritter Road
Mechanicsburg, PA 17055

Printed in the United States of America on recycled paper

First Edition

Cover design by Mark B. Olszewski

10 9 8 7 6 5 4 3 2 1

Library of Congress Cataloging-in-Publication Data

Hacker, Randi.
    How to live green, cheap, and happy : save money! save the planet! / Randi Hacker. — 1st ed.
      p. cm.
    ISBN 0-8117-2449-2
    1. Environmental policy—United States. 2. Environmental protection—United States. 3. Environmental education—United States. I. Title.
GE180.H33 1994   93-39032
363.7'0525—dc20   CIP

Table of Contents

Chapter 9: CLEAN ENOUGH   **72**

Afterword   **81**

Acknowledgments

The author wishes to thank the following:
- Rolfe Barron and Veronica Elkins for their work on this book
- Maggie Sherman for being a true-blue procrastination partner
- Carolyn Brown for trading design work for riding lessons
- Bonnie Clymer for reading with me
- Bonnie Raitt for recording "Luck of the Draw"

Vermonters figure prominently in this book because people in Vermont are the greenest, cheapest, and happiest I know. Their greenness comes from their closeness to the land. Their cheapness comes from their staunch independence. Their happiness comes from living in one of the most beautiful places on Earth.

Introduction:
Downward Mobility

Study after study shows that it's much harder now to achieve the American dream than it ever was. The income to spending ratio is way off balance. Americans are making less money and things cost more. It's no longer easy to move up the economic ladder.

The downwardly mobile lifestyle, however, is well within everyone's grasp. No matter how much—or how little—money you make, you can be downwardly mobile.

Downward mobility is the wave of the future. It's the movement toward a less opulent, more modest lifestyle. It's the realization that less is less. New publications like the *Tightwad Times* and *Pennypincher Magazine* show how to live well for less money. People everywhere are jumping on the "Spend Less" bandwagon.

And it's no wonder. The U.S. economy has never been in worse shape. We have a deficit of $4 trillion. That's $4,000,000,000,000. No matter what reduction programs politicians undertake, a $4 trillion deficit just isn't wiped out in a couple of years. As America attempts to balance its budget, Americans are in for some rough going. In these economically challenged times, downward mobility is the only real option.

This economic instability comes at the same time as a growing awareness of Earth and our relationship to it. Too many oil spills, too many contaminated water sources, too much air pollution, and too many extinctions have finally made an impression on us. We want to do less damage to our home planet.

From these two conditions a group of people have drawn the conclusion that they can save money and save Earth at the same time—downward mobility with an eco-spin. Their philosophy is simple: The greener you live, the cheaper you can live. What's good for Earth is good for the bottom line.

People everywhere are making the green, cheap transition in their own ways. Some are hard-core. They're living in cabins with no electricity and no indoor plumbing. They're growing and canning their own vegetables. They're raising and killing their own chickens.

Some people live a more mainstream green-and-cheap lifestyle. They use manual lawn mowers. They grow food for the summer and fall. They ride their bikes to work. They compost in their backyards.

Some are green-and-cheap minimalists. They use handkerchiefs instead of tissues. They grow string beans in window boxes or on their decks. They pack their own lunches in reusable bags.

No matter where on the green-and-cheap continuum these people fall, they all have one thing in common:

They're happier.

Green-and-cheap people are happier because they're less money-dependent and more Earth-aware. They can do things for themselves. Their confidence in their ability to survive outside the system is high.

Green-and-cheap people have more control over their effect on the planet. They grow pesticide-free food. They make and use their own natural cleansers. They raise their own hormone-free chickens.

Green-and-cheap people also have higher self-esteem. They feel useful and creative. They use their brains to think up new ways to save money and save Earth. They turn egg cartons into seed-starting kits. They make unique wrapping paper out of old atlas pages. They use the barter system to get what they need.

In short, green-and-cheap people are happier because they're doing less harm to themselves and to Earth. And the more they do with Earth in mind, the more connected they feel to natural rhythms, which brings real peace of mind.

Taking that first downward step can be frightening. After all, human beings have become dependent on a lot of things that can be expensive and bad for the planet. We've gotten used to electricity, cars, plastic wrap, flush toilets, and microwave dinners.

What's more, the green-and-cheap lifestyle requires a lot more work. If you're not going to hire someone to do something for you, you have to make the time to do it yourself.

But taking that first downwardly mobile step can be incredibly liberating, too. The more independent you are, the more freedom you have to control what you do, what you eat, and how you live. And the more control you have over these things, the more EC (environmentally correct) your decisions can be.

Whether you're dipping your big toe into the green-and-cheap waters for the first time or you're already hanging ten, this book is for you. You'll find information that will help you live with less and love it. You'll find interviews with green-and-cheap pioneers. You'll find tips to help you make a smooth transition into the green-and-cheap lifestyle.

Good luck and Godspeed.

Chapter 1:
Production for Reuse

In 1992 Time/Warner published *Sex*, a book by Madonna. According to *Vanity Fair*, this megacorp printed 750,000 copies—the largest number by far of any first printing—and distributed them worldwide. Three-quarters of a million tons of aluminum were used to produce the covers—none of it recycled. Five colors and five different paper stocks were used—none of them recycled. Each copy came in its own disposable Mylar wrapper. Of the twenty thousand photographs taken of Madonna for the book, only a few hundred were used. Individually wrapped audio cassettes, CDs, and music videos were released concurrently. From an absolute waste standpoint, this book made Madonna the first celebrity in history to generate as much garbage and toxic effluent as a small town.

For those of us embracing the green, cheap, and happy lifestyle, the disposable era is history. It has to be. As Earth's garbage situation careens out of control, it's up to all of us to give up our dependence on disposables.

On one hand, this will be inconvenient. No more buying whatever we want. No more unthinkingly throwing out vast quantities of garbage without regard to what happens to it. No more thinking that as long as it's out of the house or the office or the car, it's not a problem.

On the other hand, there will be less litter on the roadside and less garbage all around, including toxic and hazardous material. There will be fewer new landfills and fewer incinerators, which will lead to cleaner air and water.

It also means we'll be using our gray matter to find new ways to cut down on garbage. We can't help but come up with some clever things. A species that can invent animation, silicon chips, the fax, and liposuction can surely think of other uses for—and ways to avoid producing—future garbage.

We also have to retrain our brains to tell the difference between what we want and what we need. We see so many advertisements and so many things that other people have that it's not surprising we have a hard time distinguishing between the two. We don't take the time to think through many of our purchases. This leads to impulse purchases that generate a lot of garbage and frequently become garbage themselves.

Before we buy anything new, we need to ask ourselves the three GC&H questions:

Question #1: How much is it?

There are two levels to this question. The first is what the item will cost you. How much will you be out of pocket if you buy it?

The second level is planetary. What is the cost to Earth? What sort of natural resources were used or abused to make this item? Where will it end up once you're done with it?

Question #2: What will I do with the disposable element?

Here in the late twentieth century, pretty much everything has a disposable element, whether it's organic, as in the case of apple cores or banana peels, or synthetic, like shrink wrap or Mylar. Apple cores you might put in your compost heap or feed to a horse. In the case of the Mylar, your answer might be "I'll throw it away" or "I'll use it as wrapping paper."

Question #3: Do I need this item enough to justify its impact on my bank account and on Earth?

The answer to this question requires thinking in the long term. The blister pack containing batteries for your Walkguy will still be here one hundred years from now as litter or hazardous waste or landfill stuffing.

Perhaps the best way to get into the right frame of mind for the GC&H lifestyle is to think of Native Americans. One thing Europeans didn't find when they came here was big landfills full of Natives' garbage. Native tribes used everything. When they killed an animal for food, they used the skin for clothing, the feet for rattles, the sinew for thread, the stomach and bladder as pouches, the intestines to wrap the fat in for winter snacking. They used the bones to make needles, the brain to tan leather. They ate the meat. What they did discard was always 100 percent biodegradable. The Natives respected Earth.

Although it may be a bit harder to respect a plastic food container, we need to think along similar lines. When we look at a possible purchase, we've got to think about what we can do with every part of it. Take yogurt, for example. You eat what's inside, then what do you do with the "skin"? Toss it? Or use it as a storage unit or a beach toy or a scoop for birdseed or a flowerpot?

It would be foolish to think that we could break our disposable habit just like that. We couldn't even if we wanted to. So many things we do need come in packages that really can't be used again. But we can start looking at whatever we do buy from this neo-Native perspective. If we can't use it all at least one more time, can we use any part of it again?

Once you start to keep or use everything you buy, you'll have to buy less. No matter how creative you are, there's only a certain number of yogurt containers you can fit realistically into your life.

THE MYTH OF PLASTIC RECYCLING

Recycling is, of course, a viable alternative to throwing some things away. But it isn't the final answer to the trash problem, particularly when it comes to plastic.

Technically, plastic can't be recycled—not like glass or paper, that is. Recycling means being made back into what it was before. Glass is the ultimate recycling material. Soda bottles, ketchup bottles, and juice bottles can all be made right back into soda bottles, ketchup bottles, and juice bottles.

Because plastic picks up little particles of whatever was stored in it, soda bottles, oil jugs, and other containers can't be entirely recycled back into containers again. They can be made into ski jacket filler and carpeting and park benches. But this doesn't cut down on the amount of new plastic that has to be made for bottles. What's more, plastic park benches and ski jacket filler will eventually end up as garbage again.

When you buy plastic, you are buying future garbage. You can use it over and over again, but eventually you're going to have to throw it away.

This Is for You!

If there's one thing for sure, you will end up with too many plastic containers and bags. What do you do? Holidays and birthdays are the perfect time to get rid of your disposable excess by turning it into gift packaging. A washed Styrofoam cheese tray is the perfect Christmas cookie tray. Supermarket produce bags are just the right size for a loaf of bread. Yogurt containers are great as seedling starter or bulb-forcing pots.

The Best Way to Wash a Plastic Bag

Washing plastic bags is an icky undertaking. Wet plastic bags are slippery and sometimes slimy—not two of the most popular sensations among humans. What's more, washed plastic bags never look that clean. Still, washing them is the only way to go in the GC&H era.

Turn two bags inside out. Place one hand inside each. Using a little peppermint soap, wash the bags as if you were washing your hands. (Never use dishwashing detergent to wash a plastic bag. Dishwashing detergent has carcinogens that plastic picks up.) Rinse. Hang them upside down to dry. To cut down on that cloudy look, let your bags dry out completely before you put them away.

TOP ELEVEN GREEN AND CHEAP REUSE CONCEPTS

1. Nifty Modular Food Storage Units. Put your leftovers in old yogurt containers and label everything. It's hard to tell where last night's spaghetti is if you've got five containers that all say "vanilla yogurt."

2. The Pampered Pet Low-Impact Bowl Set. Planet-loving cats and dogs enjoy their kibbles and water in old cottage cheese containers.

3. No-Spill Glass Jar Glass. When you pack a lunch, bring your beverage in a glass jar. Screw on the lid to keep it from spilling.

4. Junk Pads. If the eighties were the era of junk bonds, the nineties are the era of junk pads. Turn scrap paper into scratch pads. Cut papers into relatively uniform size. Clip them together with a binder clip or punch holes at the top and tie with string or ribbon. Leave them by the phone, in the glove compartment, or on the kitchen counter. You'll never have to buy another notepad for the rest of your life.

5. Chinese Takeout Mini Greenhouse. When you've eaten the last morsel of Happy Family on a Sizzling Plate, turn that little foil pan and clear plastic cover into a seedling nursery. Fill it with dirt, and plant broccoli, beans, tomatoes, or whatever. Water, cover, and leave near a window. Keep the soil moist; the sun will do the rest.

6. Just Add Water Flour Paste. Flour paste is a major adhesive. When you need paste, pour some flour into a bowl, add water, mix to make a paste, and brush the paste where you need glue. Refrigerate the leftover for future use.

7. Formerly Cosmetic Gift Seed Containers. Buy lip balm, rouge, foundation, and creams in little pots. Once empty, they're perfect for seed storage. Make new labels to stick on the cover. Use your flour glue to paste them down.

8. De-Personalized Stationery. Here on Earth, there is no dearth of junk mail. A lot of it is printed on high quality paper that is a pleasure to write on—especially with a fountain pen. Put a big X through the printed part, and write letters to your friends (or creditors) on the back. Use their return envelopes, too. Just remember to cross out that bar code at the bottom

so your letter to Aunt Millie doesn't end up at the headquarters of Young Luddites for a Strong National Defense.

9. The Amazing Loofah Kitchen Scrubber. When you need a new loofah, use the old one for household duty. It really gets off scum and grime. You can even grow your own loofahs. They're a kind of gourd. Seeds are available in seed catalogs.

10. Map Wrap. Old road atlases make great wrapping paper.

11. Old Egg Carton Seed Starters and Pill Minders. Old egg cartons have two reuses:

a. Fill the sections with potting soil. Plant one seed in each. Place on a windowsill that gets plenty of light. Water regularly. Transplant your seedlings when they're an inch tall.

b. Write the name of each weekday over a section. Place the vitamins and other pills you take daily in each section. Take your pills.

How to Make Your Own Official Scrap Paper Logo

Make your junk mail stationery even cooler by turning it into official scrap paper. Here's how:

1. Take a piece of scrap paper.

2. Using a crayon, a pen, a colored pencil, or a magic marker, write the words *Official Scrap Paper* somewhere on the printed side.

3. Draw a geometric shape nearby, or enclose the words in a rectangle to create a logo.

For very little money, you can have your *Official Scrap Paper* logo made into a stamp at a local print shop. The stamp raises the eco-chic level to stratospheric levels. (For more on eco-chic, see Chapter 2.)

101 THINGS TO DO WITH BALING TWINE

Nina Tuller grew up around horses. There could be as many as twenty at one time on the family farm in Middlesex, Vermont. To get through the winter, twenty horses need to eat a great deal of hay—two thousand bales of it to be approximate. Every bale of hay is tied together with two pieces of baling twine. That's four thousand pieces of baling twine. Each piece of baling twine is about four feet long. Nina's family was in danger of being buried alive under a mountain of baling twine.

My mother gave us all baling twine and told us to invent something we needed. We didn't come up with exactly 101, but we came up with quite a few.
— *Nina Tuller*

So Nina and her six brothers and sisters made lead ropes and halters for the horses. They made belts and rugs. They made dog leashes. They even made Christmas ornaments.

"That probably saved us a lot of money," said Nina.

Most of the creations were done by braiding baling twine together. Depending on what she was making, Nina used two or three pieces per strand. She invented techniques as she went along. Nina learned macrame so she was able to make planter holders out of baling twine.

As creative as Nina and her sibs were, they never managed to use up all the baling twine they generated, but Nina is grateful to her mother for introducing her to the recycle and reuse ethic.

"It has made me more imaginative and self-reliant," says Nina.

Two Other Things to Make with Baling Twine

Now you probably wish you had at least one horse or cow so that you too could make neat stuff from baling twine. Bike over to the nearest farm and see if the owner will give you some. (Don't let him give you too much.) Invent things you need. Here are two ideas to get you started.

1. Rustic Gift Ribbon. Wrap your next gift in a map and tie it with baling twine. Savings: three dollars.

2. Low-Tech Ski Boot Carrier. Braid three pieces together. Tie the ends to make one big loop. Slip the loop through one

THE GC&H QUIZ

Come up with one use for each disposable item listed below. Calculate your savings. No answer is correct or silly. Whatever you do that isn't tossing it away is good.

1. Dry cat food bags

_____

Savings: _____
2. The fronts of used greeting cards

_____

Savings: _____
3. Water you've boiled vegetables in

_____

Savings: _____
4. The bottoms of matchboxes

_____

Savings: _____
5. Cold cereal boxes

_____

Savings: _____

Suggested answers:
1. Use them as garbage bags.
2. Write recipes on the back.
3. Water your plants with it (after it cools).
4. Line them with pieces of construction paper cut to fit and use them as frames for school photos.
5. Make a diagonal cut in them from the back top to about halfway down the front for a library-style magazine file.

set of buckles on each ski boot. Buckle the boots. Sling them over your shoulder. Savings: five dollars.

THE YARD SALE IMPERATIVE

Of course, production for reuse doesn't apply only to things you buy. It also applies to things you have and want to get rid of: clothes, old cards, old photos, light fixtures, and so forth. Have a yard sale. If you price something right, someone will buy it no matter what it is or what shape it's in. At a yard sale in Montgomery, Vermont, someone bought a broken toaster because it was only ten cents. He planned to repair it and have breakfast.

PASS IT ON

Organize a reuser exchange in your neighborhood. You can't think of everything, so share ideas on how to reuse. Exchange reusables—maybe your neighbor has a drawerful of plastic bags but needs some of those yogurt containers that are falling off your shelf.

THE WATER CYCLE

So many of us take water for granted. Yet water is one of our most valuable and necessary resources. Our wastefulness and cavalier attitude about water have resulted in a clean water shortage in many places in the United States.

If you are serious about adopting the GC&H lifestyle, you have to reevaluate your relationship with H_2O. You have to start looking at it as precious. The days of letting the tap run until the water is cold, filling a glass, drinking a sip, and pouring the rest down the drain are over. Every drop of water you collect must be used productively.

Rolfe Barron is twenty-nine. He lives in a house that has no running water in winter because his pipes freeze. Every winter morning, he walks half a mile to the spring and fills two five-gallon buckets. That's his water for the day. He uses it to wash himself, wash his dishes, water his livestock, make his coffee, and brush his teeth.

You don't have to get this radical unless you want to. But

it would be a good idea to retrain your water habits. Try this modified Rolfe routine:

Fill a one-gallon jug with water in the morning. That's your allotment for the day. You've got to make it last from brushing your teeth through cooking through drinking through washing your face before you go to bed.

Water Reuse Tips

- Water you've boiled eggs in is calcium-enriched. Use it to water your plants.
- Water you've boiled vegetables in (as long as the vegetables are pesticide-free) can be used as soup starter, to make bread, or for watering plants.
- As you run the water for your shower, collect it in a bucket for your pets, plants, or washing machine.
- Keep a jug of water in the fridge instead of running the tap when you want a cold drink.
- Don't turn on the water just to wash your hands. Wash your dishes or nylon stockings *and* your hands at the same time.

FIVE EXCUSES NOT TO REUSE

1. I'll just throw it away this once.
2. I don't have time to think of another way to use this.
3. I won't be around in one hundred years.
4. I'm too busy worrying about the present to think about the future.
5. At least I'm not littering.

FIVE REASONS TO REUSE

1. Waste will not be part of my legacy.
2. It's actually fun to think of ways to use these disposable things.
3. It makes sense.
4. It saves money.
5. It saves the planet.

Chapter 2:
Eco-Chic

Webster's Dictionary defines *chic* as a "striking but easy elegance in form or style." Green, cheap, and happy defines eco-chic as a striking but easy elegance in form or style with the planet in mind.

Those of us embracing the GC&H lifestyle are taking steps to break our fashion dependency and be less concerned about appearance. When we consider new clothes, new furniture, new stationery, or a new car, we don't judge them solely on the way they look. We consider their Resource Impact Quotient (RIQ). And the R here refers not only to natural resources but to our own cash resources as well.

The RIQ is indirectly proportional to the eco-chic level. The higher the RIQ, the lower the eco-chic level. The lower the RIQ, the higher the eco-chic level.

Four simple questions will help you determine the RIQ:

1. How much does it cost? Once again, the answer has to refer both to your cash reserves as well as to Earth's resource reserves. "Too much" means you'd feel a strain and so would the planet: high RIQ. "A lot" indicates that you could afford it but it would take a chunk out of your coffers as well as Earth's.

"A little" means it has minimum impact on all resources: low RIQ.

2. Is it secondhand? New items have a gigantic impact on Earth. Even if they are manufactured to try to minimize environmental harm, the sheer volume of new things produced contributes to planetary degradation. That's high RIQ.

Used items have less of an impact. Nothing new had to be used up in order for you to have it. Used stuff comes in less packaging—if it's packaged at all. When you buy a used item, you keep it from contributing to garbage gridlock. Quite often used things are of a much higher quality than new ones. What's more, secondhand items are always less expensive. That's low RIQ.

3. Can it be re-used? Sometimes we want to buy new things. Since hominids first walked upright on the vast African savanna, they have wanted things—a cave, a medicine bag, another mammoth. During the Victorian age, the acquisition frenzy reached new heights. Industrialization meant things could be mass-produced. Victorian houses were crowded with china dogs, vases, picture frames, and other knickknacks. Here in the twentieth century we can't expect to cut new purchases out of our lives altogether.

Can what you want to buy new last long enough to become secondhand? One test of a new item's RIQ is its durability. In a country whose government defines durable as something that will last three years, truly durable new things are not all that easy to find.

This question can also be asked of used items. Some used items have years of lifetime in them. The longer you can see your purchase serving you productively, the lower the RIQ and the higher the eco-chic level.

4. How far did it have to travel to get to you? The impact an item has on Earth is not limited only to what is used to manufacture it and what can be done once you're through with it. Transportation must also be factored in. If an item you buy comes from far away, it must have been trucked or flown to you: high RIQ. Your purchase of it would contribute to air pol-

lution and the greenhouse effect. If an item you buy comes from nearby, less fossil fuel will be burned to get it to you. So it's lower RIQ.

Thus, a kitchen table purchased at a neighborhood yard sale for ten dollars has an eco-chic level that's through the roof. It isn't new, so nothing had to be cut down or manufactured to produce it for you. (Of course, resources were used to produce it originally.) Your purchase of it prevented it from joining 1951 newspapers and hot dogs from the sixties in our overflowing landfills (yes, wieners have actually been found intact in landfills). It saved you an easy fifty dollars on the average cost of a new table. And no truck spewed diesel exhaust to bring it to you.

THE RIQ CALCULATOR CARD

The Resource Impact Quotient of an item works on a point system. The accoutrements you want receive points if they meet certain criteria and lose points if they don't. The lower the RIQ, the higher the eco-chic level of the item in question. The higher the RIQ, the lower the eco-chic level. You can calculate the RIQ of virtually any item with this card. Simply cut the two card parts out. Cut a piece of cardboard from the back of a writing tablet to the same size as the cards. Using flour paste (see Chapter 1), glue one part to each side of the cardboard. Put it in your wallet as an easy-to-reach reference.

SIDE A

The Green, Cheap, and Happy RIQ Calculator

1. How much does it cost?
   Too much   10 points
   A lot   5 points
   A little   0 points

2. Is it secondhand?
   No   10 points
   Yes   0 points

3. Can it be reused?
   No   10 points
   Yes   0 points

4. How far did it have to travel to get here?
   Thousands of miles   10 points
   Hundreds of miles   5 points
   Tens of miles or less   0 points

SIDE B

Scoring System

0 points. Snap that baby up! The eco-chic level is phenomenal. This item's impact on Earth and your bank account is minimal.

10 points. Take it or leave it. The eco-chic level is neutral. If the item is expensive and secondhand, the main impact is on your cash resources. If the item is cheap and new, the impact is on the planet. It's your call.

20 points or more. Walk away while there's still time. The eco-chic level is virtually nonexistent. Not only are you spending a lot of money, you're also using a lot of natural resources.

A DISPOSABLE MYTH

You've heard people say, "Why have it repaired? You might as well buy a new one." They were thinking convenience, not green, cheap, and happy.

Having things repaired is coming back into vogue. People are finding that it pays to fix rather than buy new for three reasons:

1. If you repair something, you're keeping it out of the garbage tsunami.

2. No matter what you think, it's going to cost less to have it repaired than it will to buy a new one. Maybe not a lot less, but definitely less.

3. Repairs are the ultimate in eco-chic. If something you've got has a patch or a peg, it is pushing the outside of the green and cheap eco-chic envelope.

THE DUCT-TAPE SOLUTION

In Vermont it's easy to wax poetic about duct tape. It's the repair tool of choice. Its usefulness is acknowledged by everyone from white-haired grandmothers to tricycle-riding tots.

Duct tape—or duck tape as it's sometimes called—is a strong, flexible, silvery gray tape that can repair virtually anything. Duct tape has been used to keep ski boots together, to repair suspenders, to hold together shattered windowpanes, to cover holes in work gloves, to darn socks. It can even work as a bandage.

Duct tape's repair advantage is that it's quick and strong. It can extend the lifespan of an item for years sometimes.

WILD FOR EARTH

We humans are vain. And we spend plenty of cash seeing to it that we look good. We condition our hair. We cream our skin. We paint our eyelids. We tuck up our sagging brows. We'll buy anything that is supposed to prevent aging.

The hair care industry produces millions of plastic containers each year. Every lipstick manufactured in this country comes in its own disposable container. The tons of moisturizer we apply comes in plastic tubes, jars, and pump bottles.

It's time to put Earth before your appearance.

Your hair may be a little less manageable because you use conditioner only every other time you wash it, but a little less pollution will end up on the planet. And you'll go through it more slowly, your supply will last longer, and you'll buy less.

ROLFE BARRON, UNFASHION ARBITER

It is six o'clock in the morning. Rolfe is walking back from the spring carrying the two five-gallon pails with his day's water. Rolfe's water-drawing ensemble consists of a pair of work pants patched in green and black wool, an old ski jacket, a pair of gloves held together by duct tape, a Raichle cap. It's clear at a glance that Rolfe is a man who knows how to wear clothes.

If fashion is what everyone is wearing, then unfashion is what no one but you is wearing. And Rolfe is the unfashion leader in his community of Montgomery, Vermont.

"When you dress green and cheap, you'll be the only person dressed the way you are," he says.

Rolfe began developing "the Rolfe look" at an early age.

"I got the retrofashion idea through skiing and camping," says Rolfe. "As a boy, I noted that the hottest skiers on the hill were often the most unfashionably dressed. And that the old clothes I wore to play in were the most comfortable. I was free to be unconcerned with their look or condition."

Every day he challenges Paris haute couture a little bit more.

"Why not put an old suitcoat to use as a work jacket? It's a question of just what you are willing to wear," he says.

Rolfe is willing to wear just about anything.

He doesn't mind that some people laugh at his outfits. He knows that when you forge a new path, some people just won't understand. He believes that unfashionability builds character.

When you make up a wardrobe entirely out of thrift-store and yard-sale clothing, you're bound to end up with things that are wildly out of date and tending toward raggedy," he says. "Neighbors and strangers may openly gawk at this scarecrow costume, but it's important to recall that your outfit is creative *and* affordable. The stronger your character, the more clothing choices open to you.

—*Rolfe Barron*

WEAR THINGS OUT
Maybe you're not yet as strong of character as Rolfe. Still, you too can be eco-chic. One of the most efficient ways to save money on clothing is to wear your old clothes until they wear out. That means if you need a new gardening coat or work pants, don't run out to buy them. Go to the back of your closet and see what's there.

Don't be tyrannized by labels or convention. If you have

an old business suit you haven't worn for years, wear the jacket when you prune the apple tree or just for casual use. It's warm, has big pockets, and will last a long time.

Old clothes have an eco-chic level that's sky high. They don't cost any money. They're used. And you don't have to burn any fossil fuel to get them. Wearing old clothes until they wear out and then repairing them and wearing them some more is perhaps the ultimate in eco-chic.

THE STORY OF EVEWEAR

Eve Gruntfest has her Ph.D. in geography. She teaches at Colorado State University. Her area of expertise is floodplains. She is flown all over the world to talk about floods and teach people not to put their homes in places that might become submerged.

When she's not in India talking about the Ganges flood basin, she's at the Salvation Army sorting through second-hand items looking for bargains.

Eve has been into used clothing since her first foray into a thrift store at the age of eighteen. At forty, she's well known in the thrift stores of Colorado Springs, and she even received a commendation from the Salvation Army for her patronage. She knows just where to go to find an $80 Neiman-Marcus blouse for $2.50.

Both the bargain basement prices and the greenness of used clothing appeal to Eve.

> **B**uying used clothing is a very recycling thing to do. Not only are you reusing the clothes themselves, but you're recycling the memories of the period that is associated with them. There's something elegant about the endless recycle cycle.
>
> —*Eve Gruntfest*

Eve is also into the thrill of the search. When she goes to a thrift store she never knows what she'll find.

"You can get quality goods secondhand," says Eve, "really exquisite stuff, often made of natural fibers."

Eve's thrifting habit regularly puts her under a mountain of used clothing. To avoid being buried alive in secondhand clothes, she started Eve's Boutique, an irregularly scheduled shopathon. A select few customers and friends are invited over to browse through Eve's collection and are encouraged to buy what they need.

"I get a real kick out of telling someone Liz Claiborne made this just for her," she laughs.

Her customers have found that the clothes they buy at Eve's Boutique can be worn virtually anywhere. In 1989, a writer for *Sports Illustrated for Kids* wore EveWear to the White House for a visit with President Bush.

"And recently," adds Eve, "a friend wore a suit she bought from me for three dollars to a court hearing and won a fifteen thousand dollar settlement." Talk about dress for success!

Eve says to introduce kids to the joy of thrifting. The low cost of secondhand clothes means that kids can have more clothing than they could if you bought new.

"Kids can have two pairs of shoes from a thrift store but only one pair new," says Eve. "When you put it to them that way, they're really into it."

Eve loves to thrift and she encourages others to join her. But she acknowledges the need for some people to buy new.

"If no one shopped at the department stores," she muses, "there'd be nothing for us to buy at the thrift stores."

Eve's Thrifting Tips

1. Don't go on a Saturday. It's an overwhelming turn-off.
2. Don't go looking for one thing. Do a survey the first time. Be flexible.
3. Look for holes and stains.
4. Always buy cashmere.

Chapter 3:
Grow It and Eat It

Things grow on Earth. No other planet we know of has this built-in feature. If you plant a seed on Mars, it will not grow. If you plant a sapling on Neptune, it will not grow. If you plant either on Earth, it will grow.

When we humans understood this, it radically altered the way we live. Instead of spending most of our time walking around looking for food, we could stay in one place and grow the food we needed. This meal management shift gave us the opportunity to create suburban housing developments, and it also had a measurable effect on our fitness (but more about that in Chapter 8).

Over the years, foods have been altered radically. Though much more produce is grown, it is not all good for you. Pesticides and fungicides are not healthy for us or the planet. Preservatives have some nasty side effects. All the impacts of irradiation and genetically engineered foods have yet to be discovered, and such foods won't always be labeled. You might not know that you're buying jam with irradiated strawberries in it or tomatoes containing mouse genes.

Never has it been so difficult to decide what's good for

you and what isn't. In addition to the ill effects on us and the ecosystem, our food tampering can be expensive. Pesticides cost money, and that cost is factored into the price you pay, as are shipping costs and packaging costs.

As always in the GC&H model, *cost* here refers not just to what you spend when you buy food. It also reflects what price Earth is paying to support your food needs. Fossil fuels burned in shipping cause air pollution and contribute to the greenhouse effect. (Some fossil fuels never even make it to the truck: Oil spills are among the most destructive—and frequent—eco-disasters in the world.) Packaging most often ends up as land-filler when it isn't blowing around in parks and on highways.

Buying asparagus out of season, for example, is costly: The spears are expensive to you and expensive to Earth because they're shipped long-distance. So in winter, learn to like cabbage.

One way to be sure that what you're eating is good for you and for Earth is to grow it yourself. Green, cheap, and happy people everywhere are rediscovering Earth's ability to provide for them. Whether they live downtown or out of town, they're seeding and weeding their own Earth victory gardens. Organic string beans and plum tomatoes are sprouting on the decks of fourth-floor walk-ups in Manhattan. Homegrown, radiation-free strawberries are turning up in the breakfast bowls of suburbia. Exurban gardens are producing enough no-pesticide sweet corn and zucchini to feed whole counties.

Growing your own food is the cheapest way to eat in these troubled eco-times. A twenty-dollar investment in seeds in the spring will yield you food that, if handled properly, could last you well into the winter.

What's more, growing your own food gives you the independent edge. Our world is going through a tremendous upheaval. Governments are toppling. Financial crises are erupting all over. War, revolution, and devastating natural disasters are commonplace. All this is bound to have a disruptive effect on the economy. The more you can do yourself, the less the fluctuating consumer price index concerns you.

THE FIFTH FOOD GROUP

Grain. Fruit and vegetables. Dairy. Protein. Chemicals. The food we buy is loaded with chemicals whose effects are not always predictable. Not all of them are bad for you, but some can cause allergic reactions and, in children, hyperactivity.

Here's a list of some potentially harmful additives that regularly appear in the foods we buy. Consider cutting them out of your diet.

- Acesulfame K. This sweetener used in chewing gum, dry beverage mixes, instant coffee and tea, gelatin desserts, puddings, and nondairy creamers causes cancer in animals and was inadequately tested by the FDA.
- Artificial colorings. Food dyes are strictly cosmetic. They're used to keep food looking fresh even when it's not. Synthetic food dyes are suspected carcinogens.
- Aspartame. This artificial sweetener is suspected of causing altered brain function in users and is known to cause mental retardation in infants who are unable to metabolize phenylketonuria, an amino acid found in aspartame. A rat study also found an increased risk of brain tumors.
- Nitrate and nitrite. Sodium nitrite and sodium nitrate are meat preservers and have been used for centuries. Nitrate is harmless but is easily converted by bacteria into nitrite. Nitrite can form nitrosamines, which have been connected with stomach cancer.

Look at the labels and avoid foods that contain the above.

ONE WOMAN'S GARDEN

Marie LaPre Grabon spends weeks in late winter and early spring sketching her garden. Where the endive goes and where the lettuce grows are esthetic as well as practical decisions. The plants are arranged to make a pleasing pattern.

Marie began gardening after her divorce. Living in the suburbs with her four kids, she suddenly felt an urge to plant a garden. So she dug a plot in her suburban Boston backyard and planted seeds.

She didn't start out with the goal of feeding herself and her kids. It was more a desire for a spiritual connection.

"I didn't get very much food," she said, "but it gave me a lot of satisfaction. It was a part of becoming independent and a part of giving the kids a sense of independence, too."

Marie keeps track of all her garden plans and plants in a spiral notebook. Journal entries record planting dates, locations, weather conditions, and the progress of the seedlings as they grow into mature plants. Stuck between pages are seed envelopes, seed catalogs, and a pencil sketch of the garden as she has laid it out.

"I recommend journal keeping to anyone starting a garden," advises Marie.

After the planning phase comes the hard work. Seeding, weeding, watering, and protecting the plants are time-consuming but pleasurable undertakings for Marie.

"I love maintaining the garden," she says. "My garden is basically better kept and better maintained than my house. I get such satisfaction from being in the sun, playing in the dirt with insects buzzing around me. I spend a tremendous amount of time making everything look just so. I think of it as a big, never-finished painting."

Issues of life and death come with gardening. You've done a lot of hard work to raise this food, but you don't want other animals to eat it. So how do you keep other animals out? A fence will keep out the bigger ones, but insects don't pay much attention to fences. When Marie's potato patch becomes a potato bug social club, she kills them by hand.

"I turned it into a ritual," she says. "Each year I choose two rocks as my potato bug eliminators and I keep them in a special place. Every day I go into the garden and squish potato bugs between them."

By late summer, Marie's garden is producing more food than she can possibly eat. Then it's time to get down to putting some away for winter. She dries herbs, cans tomatoes, and pickles cucumbers at a frenzied pace. Fresh vegetables won't wait, and the job can be overwhelming, but for Marie there's something compelling her to steam, freeze, cut, and can.

"Most people are deprived of making things with their own hands," said Marie. "Gardening and canning empower me, and that's part of the attraction."

What's more, there's the future to think of.

When we sit down to dinner and it's chicken from our barn and vegetables from our garden and they're all healthful—that's a wonderful feeling.

—Marie LaPre Grabon

Marie's Gardening Guidelines

Before you get out the trowel, read through these hints:

1. Gather information before you begin so you're not just guessing at gardening procedure. Purchase a basic gardening book.

2. Start modestly. If you don't contain your enthusiasm, you could end up with more than you bargained for—too much food. It's better to have less than you need at first than too much. You can always expand next year.

3. Make the chemical decision before you plant. Decide just how much—if any—chemical interference you will accept.

4. Expect some surprises. Some plants may not yield any food. Some may yield too much. Surely you've heard the gardener's end-of-season lament: "I wish my zucchini plant would die."

5. Don't be afraid to get dirty. Garden dirt is not bad for you.

THE GARDEN JOURNAL

Keep your own garden journal. Record what you've planted, what you got, what you want to plant next year. Your journal will give you a record of what worked and what didn't. It will help you and your garden evolve.

Here are Marie's suggestions on how to get your journal started:

1. Write anything. Your journal does not have to be solely about the garden. Include any observations you want.

2. Sketch things out. Draw what you want your garden to look like. Sketch the seedlings. Draw a tomato.

3. Note the weather.

4. Include what didn't work as well as what did. Knowing what won't grow will help you succeed next year.

5. Include feelings as well as facts.

There is a sample ledger sheet on the next page to get you started.

BEAN GROWING MADE EASY

No matter where you live, you can grow beans. Beans will grow anywhere, from large garden plot to third-grade classroom. They're hardy. They're prolific. They're nutritious. Even if you just grow enough for one meal, it's a start.

What you need:
- a one-quart yogurt container
- dirt
- pebbles
- bean seads

What you do:

1. Punch three small holes in the bottom of the yogurt container. Invert the lid and put it under the container to catch the overflow water.

2. Place a layer of small pebbles on the bottom.

3. Fill the yogurt container with soil.

4. Poke three one-inch-deep holes in the soil with your index finger.

5. Place one bean seed in each hole. Cover it lightly with dirt.

6. Water whenever the soil is dry.

7. When the seedlings are about one inch high, transplant them to a garden or a bigger pot. As the bean plants grow, they'll need something to twine around. Put a stick in the pot or run a string from the pot to the window frame. Keep the window open whenever possible.

THE GC&H HOME HARVEST LEDGER

Vegetable_____

Date planted _____   Harvest Date _____

Flavor _____   Yield _____

Comments_____

_____

Vegetable_____

Date planted _____   Harvest Date _____

Flavor _____   Yield _____

Comments_____

_____

Vegetable_____

Date planted _____   Harvest Date _____

Flavor _____   Yield _____

Comments_____

_____

Vegetable_____

Date planted _____   Harvest Date _____

Flavor _____   Yield _____

Comments_____

_____

8. Harvest the beans.

9. Always leave at least one bean pod on the plant to mature. Use those seeds for next year's planting.

Beans in the Year 2000

Storing food for future eating is a time-consuming job, but worth it. The hours spent preserving really pay off in the pleasure you'll get eating food from your own garden in January.

There are different ways to put food by. One of the quickest is freezing. Here's a simple way to have beans well into the winter.

1. Wash your beans.

2. Slice them on the diagonal into two-inch pieces.

3. Fill a big pot with water and bring to a boil.

4. Boil beans for three minutes.

5. Using a slotted spoon, remove beans and plunge them into very cold water.

6. Spread beans on cloth and let them dry.

7. Freeze in a bag. You should be able to pour out individual portions because dry beans will not freeze together into one big lump.

A WORD ABOUT MEAT

Many green people are cutting meat out of their diets altogether. When it comes to beef, this makes good eco-sense. Hundreds of acres of rain forest are being turned into grazing areas for beef cattle. And in the western United States, cattle are destroying millions of acres of public grasslands.

There are good reasons to cut out commercially raised chickens, too. Most chickens are raised in overcrowded pens where they have to fight for food and often end up pecking and injuring each other.

It takes a lot of water to produce meat. In fact, it takes a hundred times more water to produce a pound of beef than it does to produce a pound of wheat. And commercial broiler operations are water-intensive, too. Both chickens and cattle are given hormones and other drugs, which are passed on to us when we eat them.

Red or white, meat comes prepackaged—shrink-wrapped on polystyrene trays. Polystyrene trays can sometimes be recycled, but they still contribute to the demise of our ozone layer. And the shrink wrap adds to our ever-growing garbage gridlock.

Humans are omnivores, however, which means we'll eat anything. And if you are going to eat meat, raising your own is the greenest way to do it. Many green people are raising their own chickens, which are easier to raise than cattle. Home-raised chickens are healthful (no hormones) and can have as decent a life as you give them.

Home-raised chickens aren't as resource gobbling, either. They can be given the water you run for your shower. They eat almost anything you don't, except citrus peel. No fossil fuel has to be burned to get them to your table.

Chicken can be placed in a deep freeze in clean, used plastic bags, or it can be canned in reusable glass jars. The way you choose to preserve the meat is up to you.

Chapter 4:
Free Trade Acts

In 1990 there was approximately $246 billion worth of currency—bills and coins—circulating in the United States. In Fort Knox and in the basement of the Federal Reserve Bank in New York City there rests approximately $11 billion in gold ingots. Thus, about $235 billion worth of currency is worthless, in a sense. In fact, the whole concept of currency works because no one cares whether there's anything precious behind the money as long as the money is accepted.

This is not news. Use of currency has pretty much been an act of faith for years. Throughout economic history more paper money has been printed than there is gold—or another item of value—to back it up. Way back when, people who had gold gave it to goldsmiths to hold. The goldsmiths placed the gold in their safes and issued a receipt to the owner. The owner could use the receipt to purchase things. The goldsmiths also loaned (with interest) the worth of this gold to other people and gave them receipts (a form of currency) to spend.

The use of currency replaced the trade system for two important reasons:

1. Currency was much easier to carry and spend than, say, a goat.

2. The value was commonly agreed upon.

No need to debate the relative values of a cow and a coat for trade. Consumers simply agreed upon a price and then paid the equivalent in currency. People thought this setup was great.

When you think about it, though, convenience is the only real advantage of currency and it's debatable whether easy spending is, in fact, an advantage. The fluctuating value of currency causes inflation and makes us lose sight of the true cost of our purchases and worth of our work. The $4 trillion U.S. debt is a fairy tale number. It's so vast, we can't conceive of how much it is. It's going to make the economy and our currency unstable for a long time.

Green, cheap, and happy people are making the transition from economics to "eco"-nomics. They're breaking their dependency on currency by using the barter system—the exchange of goods and services among providers.

People have been using the barter system in some way for thirty-five thousand years. Cro-Magnons traded amber for grain. Medieval merchants traded wool for wheat. Contemporary governments trade arms for hostages. When you barter, you come face to face with the real value of something. A dollar is not always a dollar but a goat is always a goat.

The Internal Revenue Service does expect you to report the fair market value of what you've traded—especially if it's a material object such as a car or a stove. When you trade services, the "income" is harder to assess. By law, if you don't report your barters and you are caught, you will be penalized, and if you're audited, one of the first things you'll be asked is if you did any bartering. It's up to you to decide what and how much to declare.

Green, cheap, and happy people are bringing back the barter system in a big way. They're trading skills for services, services for luxuries, and luxuries for skills. And they're finding that trading works on many levels.

- It develops community strength. Members of a community have different skills. Some are carpenters. Some
  are bookkeepers. Some are handy with needle and
  thread. Others bake delicious bread. Still others can
  do accounting or give legal advice. Get to know the
  skills of your neighbors, and discover whom you can
  rely on for what. When your neighbors, in turn, know
  what they can rely on *you* for, you all will benefit.
- It develops individual skills. When you offer your services, you need to feel confident that what you do is
  worth something. Whatever your skills are, the more
  they are called upon, the better you become at them.
- It builds self-esteem. You have to assess yourself honestly to decide what your skills are worth. You don't
  want to feel you haven't gotten an equal exchange. Bartering asks you to take a good look at yourself and
  determine what you do best. And when you feel com-
  petent, your self-esteem soars.
- It fosters independence. The more you can do yourself, the less you have to rely on the ups and downs of
  our economy. The stronger the barter foundation you
  and your neighbors establish, the more self-sufficient
  you will all feel.
- It saves you money. When you trade, the money you
  don't spend stays in your bank account. You'll have
  more money to pay for things you can't barter for.
- It has a certain subversive satisfaction. When you exchange services for services, it's almost as if you've
  gotten something for free, although the IRS does expect
  you to report barter on your tax returns.

ON-THE-JOB TRAINING
Bartering doesn't always have to be the exchange of one con-
crete thing for another. You can barter your time, working
alongside someone who has a skill you want to learn. This is
good for two reasons:

1. You'll get what you want—a barn, a house, some interior work.

2. You'll learn a new skill that you can use in the future either for barter or for yourself.

Learning other skills is another way to free yourself from dependence on our currency economy. The more things you can do for yourself, the more stable your home economy can be.

MAGGIE SHERMAN, BARTER QUEEN

Maggie Sherman is an artist living in northern Vermont. Art does not provide the steadiest of incomes. In the two decades Maggie has been selling her art and art concepts, she's honed the art of barter to a fine edge.

Maggie has traded for many of the things she now has. She baked bread in exchange for faxing privileges. She gave cake in exchange for marketing consultation. She created a stuffed anatomy-chart-in-a-box for her doctor in exchange for a hernia procedure.

The barter she is perhaps most proud of is the one she orchestrated for the birthing of her son. In 1981, when she was pregnant with Andrew, she had very little money and no health insurance. She organized a trade with her obstetrician.

"I was making banners at the time," explained Maggie. "I asked the doctor if she'd consider bartering her services for a banner."

The doctor agreed to a half-and-half arrangement—half art, half cash.

Maggie cast a friend's face and hands and a foot in plaster gauze. She also cast a child's face, hands, and foot. She collected a large piece of fabric from a salvage store and turned it all into a wall hanging.

"Bartering for Andrew's birth saved me about four hundred dollars," said Maggie.

Maggie thinks bartering is the way to conduct business whenever possible.

I haven't met with any negatives, really. Most people are interested. They find a novelty element in the suggestion of barter. It spices up their lives a bit and gives them a good story to tell.

—*Maggie Sherman*

Maggie's Tips for First-Time Barterers

The barter system forces us to think about fairness. You have to work out exchanges that are fair to you and to the person you're bartering with. Here are a few guidelines from Maggie to help you ease into the bartering routine.

- Don't be afraid to ask. Most people are really fascinated by the novelty of a barter. You never know who'll say yes. And the worst they can do is say no.
- Be realistic. Think about your abilities. Don't offer to build someone's chimney if you don't know anything about stonemasonry.
- Barter your strengths. If signmaking is your area, make signs. The better you are at what you do, the more you can barter for it.
- Barter your pleasures. What you do, you'll do in your spare time. You don't want to procrastinate and miss your deadline or do a poor job. Your neighbors then won't want to barter with you.
- Don't undercut yourself. Assess honestly the value of your work. It will take practice. At first you may make trades that aren't really barter-efficient for you. But you'll learn as you go.
- Approach each trade individually. No universal barter standard can be set. It's something you have to work out with your trade partners. There are always several factors to figure in: season, deadline, need, etc. Five whole wheat breads and a chicken might be worth a lot more in the winter when food is scarcer than in the summer.

- Be confident in what you are offering. You've got to give the person to whom you're offering the barter the feeling you're worth it.
- Keep it light, but not too light. You've got to make the person you're bartering with see that you're serious.
- Know what you want in return. It's best to enter a barter situation with a clear idea of what it is you want out of the trade, not just what it is you're willing to trade yourself.

TRUE TRADES

What you barter for is limited only by your imagination and chutzpah. Think of a trade you would like to make and try to set it up. Here are few true-life barter stories to get you started.

- Horseback riding for legal advice. For getting two hours of contract work and consulting on financial matters, I gave an equestrian lawyer two horseback rides.
- Skiing for carpentry. After Rolfe Barron built his house, he needed someone to help him finish the inside. He got a construction engineer to do the work in exchange for telemark skiing lessons.
- Babysitting for massage. Jackie Kaufman needed some massage therapy. She traded babysitting services with the local masseuse. Jackie got two massages, and the masseuse spent a romantic, kid-free weekend away with her husband.
- Chimney cleaning for a season ski pass. Robert Worthington, a chimney sweep, cleans the local ski resort's restaurant chimneys in exchange for season ski passes for himself and his family.
- Video rentals. I belong to a video club and have occasionally ordered films I find I don't want to watch again and again. My local video store takes my rejects in exchange for free rentals.
- Art for taxes. When her taxes came due, Carolyn Brown worked it out with her accountant to exchange an original color drawing for a discount in the cost of prepar-

ing her tax returns. The fact that even accountants enter into barter agreements should convince you that it is something the IRS recognizes as legit.

HOW TO START A TRADE NETWORK

You don't know what wealth of trade talent there is in your neighborhood until you meet with your neighbors. Talk to

---

Vol. 1   **No.1**   **Spring Edition**

The Trade Paper

It's Better to Barter

The Trade Paper *is dedicated to bringing the latest trades to the community. Check our listings to see what barters you can arrange.*

• Will barter fresh bread for help weeding garden. Please contact Anne 555-1212

• Art offered in exchange for accounting services. If you would like an original painting and can do taxes, please call me. Steve 555-4343

• Work for work needed. I will help you build something of your choice if you will help me by caring for my pets while I am out of town. Call Daniel 555-0987

• Baby-sitting barter. I will take care of your kids if you will let me do laundry at your house. Please call me before my dirty clothes overrun my hamper. Irene 555-9897

The Trade Paper is published by the *Better to Barter Community Group* and distributed free to members. Dues are $5. a year. $1.00 to non-members. To place a trade ad, call 555-6754. $.50 per line.

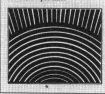

• Will barter computer services for house cleaning. If you need anything from spreadsheets to word processing done on computer and are willing to come vacuum and dust, call me. Gib 555-3456

• Riding lessons offered in exchange for house sitting. If you will stay at my house for a week while I'm gone, I will give you two English riding lessons. Call Sharon 555-4820

your friends. See if they're interested in starting up a trade network. If they are, decide on a venue, time, and place.

At the meeting, describe why the barter system is something worth investigating. Talk about the economic advantages. Then discuss who can do what and who needs what done in return. Set dues. Make a member list with phone numbers and general skills.

You might also want to start a trade newsletter. For a small fee, parties interested in bartering can list their names, numbers, and barter specialties. The more people who know about the barter system, the better for everyone.

The IRS has special rules governing barter exchanges. It would be a good idea to talk to an accountant before starting up a trade network of your own.

Chapter 5:
Just Do It (Yourself)!

As control freaks, we humans have tried to dominate virtually everything we've come across—rivers, oceans, forests, other species, and other humans. When we find we can't control something (such as the weather) by main force, we try to predict its behavior in an effort to promote the illusion that if we don't control it, at least we understand it.

This causes us to do some silly things. We build our houses in floodplains, for example, and then we are indignant when heavy rains turn the basement into a swimming pool.

It would be good for us to accept the reality of life on Earth: There are some things we can't control, no matter how much we would like to. Even if billions of dollars are poured into scientific research or new technology, we will still be powerless in certain situations. We will also be a lot poorer.

There are, however, many things we can control. Most of them affect our lives at a very basic level. Green, cheap, and happy people learn to channel their control urges into their own lives. Whether they are buying organic food at the local market or killing their own chickens out back with a sharp axe, they are taking control of how they live.

There are basically two control options for taking care of ourselves and Earth: direct and indirect.

Indirect control kicks in mainly when you shop. Although you're not in control of the making of the product, you control what you buy by making sure that it's good for you and good for the planet.

Direct control is cheapest and greenest, though it's definitely not the easiest. When you do everything for a project— whether it is building a house or cooking chicken soup—you control the quality and the cost. You can consider your health, the health of Earth, and the health of your bank account in every decision: Is the wood you use plentiful and logged responsibly? Are the chickens you will eventually cook healthy and happy?

No matter where we live, we all have direct control over some things in our lives. We can grow our own food, make our own clothes, bake our own bread, change our own oil—to name just a few things. Each one requires some knowledge, a time commitment, and a keen grasp of reality.

I'm not suggesting that we do all things for ourselves. That would promote unemployment and deprive us of the pleasures of specialization. The ability to buy things we need from other people gives us a way to get others to do the work we don't like.

But to live the green, cheap, and happy lifestyle, you must do some things for yourself. What those are is up to you. Only you can decide just what you are willing to do from scratch and what products or services you want someone else to do from scratch for you.

LINDA MARKIN ON DOING EVERYTHING YOURSELF
Linda Markin is controller at Concept II, the Vermont-based manufacturer of state-of-the-art rowing machines and oars. Out behind the house Linda Markin shares with her partner,

Marie LaPre Grabon, stands a structure casually referred to as "the barn." In fact, it's a chicken house you might consider living in. It's got heat, electricity, and finished exterior walls. Linda built it and wired it herself. It cost her two thousand dollars.

For Linda, doing things herself is a way of life as well as a way to save money. She's been at it since she graduated—broke—from Dartmouth in 1977. Over the years, she has worked closely with builders, bike repairers, and wood-carvers. She has learned to build houses, do wiring and plumbing, repair her own bicycle, build her own furniture, and carve her own utensils. Doing things herself—from the smallest project to the most complex—gives Linda the independent edge. And she's not romantic about it.

"I don't always get a better product," she says. "That's not why I do it. I do it because it's cheap and it's fun and I get a sense of satisfaction in doing it myself. I enjoy the whole process."

Linda recognizes the difference between being a perfectionist and doing the job right.

"Not insisting on perfection is reasonable," she says, "but it's not okay to do something half-assed. You've got to give it your best."

One of the most important lessons Linda has learned about doing things yourself is not to give up too early. If she finds herself at an impasse, she consults books and other people to work out the problem. Then she goes on.

"It's important to me to try really hard to figure out a solution on my own first," reflected Linda. "Doing something myself from start to finish gives me an incredible sense of accomplishment."

Linda knows that error is part of the do-it-yourself process. She has made some memorable mistakes. After she had hooked up all the wires for her barn project, she found the last two lights wouldn't go off when she flipped the switch. She had to rip out all the wiring and start over because she had used the wrong wire.

Linda determines what projects will fit in her executive schedule and undertakes only those that she can commit herself to. Doing things herself has helped strengthen Linda's self-esteem.

"It's connected with feeling adult and meeting my own needs," she says. "What I feel is a sense that I can tackle any problem. That doesn't mean I can do everything, but I know where to begin, who to call. It's helped my problem-solving skills one hundred percent."

She advises people to just try. Rather than worry in advance that it won't turn out well, take the plunge and see what happens.

You don't have to know everything before you get started. You just have to start. It's not that complicated. You can make mistakes, certainly, but nothing is forever.

—Linda Markin

FOUR TIPS FOR TAKING CONTROL

Anthropologically speaking, it hasn't been that long since doing everything for ourselves was the rule. It's only in the last century that we haven't had to split our own wood or sew our own clothing. Keep these thoughts in mind as you tap into our collective ancestral memory:

1. Expect to make mistakes. One hundred years is, after all, one hundred years. We haven't exercised the do-it-yourself part of our gray matter for a long itme. Think things through as well as you can, then try. You'll learn from your mistakes.

2. Ask for help. If you're really unsure about a part of the process, read a book about it or see if you can work alongside someone who knows.

3. Put the emphasis on function. It doesn't have to be esthetically pleasing. The measurement of success is whether it works.

4. Be creative. One of our best traits as humans is our cleverness. We're good at inventing things. So use your creativity to accomplish your tasks.

QUESTIONS TO ASK YOURSELF FIRST
Before you rush out to buy a plot of land and design and build your own house, think about these things:
- Is this a realistic project for your geographic area? If you live on West 75th Street, raising chickens is not a viable choice. But you *can* grow string beans in a window box.
- Do you have the time to commit to this project? It takes a lot longer to bake a loaf of bread than it does to buy one at the grocery store.
- Are you there spiritually? Maintaining a clear connection to the Earth-positive aspects of doing the project yourself is critical. It's what will help you put the time and effort in even if you're tired.
- Will it cost less if you do it yourself? From a savings account perspective, things generally cost less if you do them yourself. From a planetary perspective, one person making bread at home is one less person bringing home a plastic bread bag to throw away. And on a winter afternoon, having the oven on means a nice warm kitchen even if the thermostat is set low.
- Are you afraid of physical labor? Doing things yourself almost always involves physical labor. From weeding your window box garden to bringing water from the spring, you will get more exercise doing things for yourself. This is good. We sleep better, we eat better, and we feel better when we do physical labor. What's more, physical labor keeps you fit. For more on the cheapest and greenest way to pump up, see Chapter 8.

THINGS TO DO YOURSELF
This is just a partial list. Be creative and add your own items to it.

1. Raise chickens.
2. Fix your bike.
3. Bake bread.
4. Make glue.
5. Make pancakes from scratch.
6. Build a toolshed.
7. Grow your own food.
8. Clean house.
9. Tan leather.
10. Change your oil.
11. Sharpen your knives.
12. Can your own food.
13. Split wood.
14. Make maple syrup.
15. Make your lunch.
16. Brew your own beer.
17. Knit a sweater.
18. Darn your socks.
19. Make a pizza from scratch.
20. Build shelves.

21. _____

22. _____

23. _____

24. _____

25. _____

26. _____

27. _____

28. _____

29. _____

30. _____

ROLFE'S MEDITATION ON KILLING CHICKENS

Killing your own food puts you face to face with the fact that you are eating another living being in a way that buying meat from the supermarket freezer doesn't. If you raise meat, you learn to understand and accept your carnivorous nature in a new way. Here are Rolfe's thoughts on the act.

"Let's face it, folks. If you're going to eat meat, there's got to be some killing going on, whether by someone else or by you. Getting in touch with this, that is, doing the killing myself, raised all sorts of interesting issues for me on the concept of death itself. I started asking myself questions such as 'What is it that leaves a body upon death?' 'What is the soul? the life-force?'

"Whatever it is, it's frightening to me that I have the power to take it away from this animal. Does this make me a power-hungry murderer or a hungry human in search of food?"

I remember that I gave these chickens a good life—a lot of space to move around in, good food, fresh air, even a view! And I calmly resign myself to killing my own meat.

—Rolfe Barron

AN EASY BREAD RECIPE

Baking your own bread is an easier place to start than killing a chicken. The kneading of the dough is therapeutic. The sight of bread rising by a warm oven or in the sun is soothing to the soul. The smell of bread baking is heavenly.

It isn't that hard, either. Bread is difficult to ruin. As long as you don't kill the yeast, you'll end up with an edible loaf. Since most yeast deaths result from water that is too hot, the best way to avoid yeasticide is to test the water with your own hand. If it feels warm and comforting to you, the yeast will like it, too.

What's more, you can add pretty much anything to

bread—leftover bananas, old cheese (as long as it's not moldy), sour milk, grated squash, sesame seeds. The more you add, the more nutritious the bread.

Here's a basic bread recipe. Experiment with it. If you don't like it, feed it to the birds.

- In a bowl, mix 1 tablespoon of dry yeast with 2 cups of warm water (between 105 and 110 degrees F.) and 1 tablespoon of sugar, maple syrup, or honey. Let stand for 5 minutes until yeast bubbles.
- Add 1 tablespoon of salt and 5 to 6 cups of unbleached flour (one cup at a time). When the dough is too thick to stir, dump it onto a lightly floured surface. Adding flour as necessary, knead until the dough is smooth and elastic: Push the ball of dough, fold it, and give it a quarter turn, push again, fold-turn-push ... Fun, right? Kneading makes everyone happy and develops major forearms.
- Wash your bowl and coat the inside lightly with olive oil. Turn the dough in the bowl once to coat it with oil.
- Cover the bowl with a towel. Let the dough rise in a warm place for an hour or so.
- Sprinkle cornmeal on a cookie sheet.
- Punch the dough down, knead for about 5 minutes, then divide in half and form two loaves.
- Place the loaves on the cookie sheet. Cover with a towel and let them rise for 45 minutes.
- Place a pan of boiling water in the bottom of your oven. Bake your bread at 500 degrees for 10 minutes and 400 degrees for another 10 minutes. The loaves should sound hollow when you knock on the crust.
- Take the loaves off the cookie sheet and let them cool in the oven as it cools down.

HOW TO BRAIN TAN YOUR OWN LEATHER

This is not an activity for everyone. It really pushes the outside of the squeamishness envelope. But if you're brave enough it's worth it. The leather you make will be soft and top quality. It's a fact that most hunters discard the deerskin. Talk to a hunter you know and ask him or her to give you the deer hide. While you're at it, ask the hunter for the deer's head, too.

- Scrape all the fat and meat from the skin.
- Soak your hide in a solution of wood ash and water for two days. Use a twenty-gallon galvanized metal garbage can one-half full of water. Add a two-gallon bucketful of wood ash. Be careful not to get the solution on your skin.
- Meanwhile, using a bone saw, cut through the deer skull just behind the ears and scoop out the brains with a spoon.
- Blend one cup of deer brains with two cups of water. Boil. Set aside.
- Scrape the hair off the deer hide.
- Stretch the hide on a wooden frame and let it dry.
- Scrape until the skin has a parchment-like look and feel.
- Using your hands, work the skin in the brain solution. When it's saturated, roll the skin in a piece of plastic. Leave overnight.
- Stretch the wet skin on the frame and scrape to remove excess brain solution.
- Unfasten wet skin. Scrape on rope, scrape on scraper, stretch, and generally keep the fibers moving constantly until the skin is dry.
- Make a vest.

Chapter 6:
Golden Oldies

Long ago, the Cherokee people say, there were not many stars in the sky. In those days, the people ground their corn and stored it in baskets around their village. This corn fed them all winter long.

One winter morning, when the people went to their corn storage area, something was wrong.

"Someone has been stealing our corn," said a man.

"Someone big!" said a woman. "Look!"

The tracks of some giant animal could be seen in the snow. The people followed them. They led off into the forest and up a hill. At the top, they simply disappeared.

The people returned to their village and consulted the Beloved Woman, their leader. She was old and wise.

"I must see these tracks," she said when the people had told her the story.

Beloved Woman studied the tracks. She walked around them. She knelt in the snow and measured them with her hands. At last she spoke.

"These are the tracks of a giant dog," she said. "But it is a *dog like no dog on Earth. It has come from some other world and it may have great power. We must be very careful."*

"But if it continues to eat our corn, we'll starve!" cried a man.

"What can we do?" asked a woman.

"We can make a great noise," said Beloved Woman. "We can frighten the dog so that it will never return to bother us again."

The people thought this was a good plan. They went home and collected rattles and drums. Then they hid themselves near the corn storage place and waited. It was a cold, clear night, and the few stars in the sky twinkled. Elder Sister, the Moon, shone her silvery light on the snowy Earth.

Soon the people saw a great dog coming across the fields. Some of them were frightened and wanted to run, but the wise old woman whispered to them, "Wait for my signal."

The giant dog came closer. When it reached the corn stores, it began to eat. It filled its huge mouth with the white cornmeal.

"Now!" shouted Beloved Woman.

All the people beat on their drums and shook their rattles. The noise was loud as thunder. The great dog jumped up and started running. The people chased it, beating their drums and shaking their rattles. As the dog ran, cornmeal spilled out of its mouth.

The huge dog ran until it came to the top of the hill. Then it leapt into the sky and continued running until it could no longer be seen. Each grain of cornmeal that spilled from its mouth became a star. All the stars became the Milky Way—gil'liutsun stanun 'yi in Cherokee, which means "the place where the dog ran."

As the wise old woman promised, the big dog never came to bother the people again.

Native Americans had special respect for their elders. In the story, the oldest woman is not only beloved but also revered. Her advice is sought and followed. Things turn out well for the people.

These days, we treat our elders pretty badly. We ignore

them and we fear them because they remind us of our own destiny.

This is too bad, because today's elder population is unique: They are Depression survivors. They lived through a time when the conveniences we take for granted weren't available. They learned to do without resources we often waste extravagantly. Many of them had no electricity or running water. They didn't all have cars and phones. Supermarkets were still unknown.

They learned to be self-sufficient, cost-conscious, conservation-minded, and creative. Many of them made do with very little. They worked every day to meet their basic survival needs—food and shelter.

Green, cheap, and happy people understand that the future we are moving toward could be very much like the past the elders lived through—lower energy and lower tech. The skills they developed when resources and energy were difficult to procure can help us cope when resources and energy are running out. They used less gasoline because of rationing. We will have to use less gasoline because there isn't that much oil left.

That's why green, cheap, and happy people are making the elder connection. They're drawing on the past experience of elders to help them move into the future. Talking and listening to elders in their families and communities, they're rediscovering better and cheaper ways to live on Earth.

AGATHA AND WARREN BLODGETT, VERMONT ELDERS

When Agatha (pronounced uh-GAH-thuh) and Warren were kids, survival wasn't taken for granted. Indoor plumbing was not standard. Electricity wasn't included. Currency was scarce.

Yet both Agatha's and Warren's families had food to eat, places to live, and clothing to wear. And they didn't really feel deprived in any way.

"We made do with almost nothing," said Agatha. "It wasn't poverty. We had nothing and neither did anyone else."

Agatha was the daughter of the town doctor. Driving his

horse and buggy and later his car ("though he kept the horse for bad weather"), Dr. Keelan took care of the health needs of the town. Nobody had any money so he took his payment in whatever they had—ham, bacon, wood, syrup, apples, a chicken, or laundry services.

"One family who had a sick child for quite a long time made us dinner every Saturday night," said Agatha. "We'd go over and pick up hot rolls, baked beans, and maple sugar cake."

Warren's family lived on a dairy farm. Every morning he'd milk the cows, feed the livestock, and do chores before school. He wore the same outfit for a week and washed it and himself on weekends. Warren's farmhouse had indoor plumbing only because his mother traded her house in town for a bathroom and shower, installed.

"We had no electricity," said Warren. "We'd butcher our pigs, then wrap the meat in newspaper and store it in a trunk on our porch over winter."

Both of them remember their families doing pretty much everything themselves. Clothes were sewn and repaired. Bread was baked. Cottage cheese was made. Food was put by.

"My mother canned everything," says Agatha. "Peas, carrots, beets, beef, corn, jams, and jellies. It took easily a month of her time. There must have been four hundred jars in the basement. They got us clear through the winter."

Rarely did either of them get anything new. That required currency, and they didn't see much of that. At Christmas, Agatha got two gifts—one fun, one practical.

"When I got a new pair of shoes, I knew someone must have paid my father in cash," says Agatha.

For the most part, they made do with what they had. One of the things they had to do was make repairs. And they found out that repairing things made sense—financially and practically. Take the manure spreader. One of Warren's boyhood jobs was fertilizing the fields. This required a lot of time and effort to do by hand.

"We had a perfectly good horse-drawn manure spreader

under the shed just waiting to be fixed," said Warren. "So I fixed it."

One of the most valuable lessons Agatha and Warren learned was that just because you *needed* something didn't mean you would get it.

"We didn't buy anything until we had saved enough to buy it," said Agatha.

Both Warren and Agatha lived closer to nature. Everything was used. Warren fed leftovers to the pigs and chickens. When the milk and cream were separated and sold, the skim was used to make cottage cheese. Water that had been used to boil potatoes was used in bread. Even the autumn leaves were "recycled." Agatha remembers piling them against the foundation of the house to help insulate it. Her father built a special fence to keep the leaves in place.

"We had holes in that house we could throw a cat through," remembers Agatha. "The leaves really kept us warmer." Warren notes that spruce boughs work well in this capacity, as do bales of hay.

In those days, ecology was not on their minds. It was just in their lifestyle.

We may not have been consciously green, but we were cheap and happy.

—Agatha Blodgett

ELDERS—WHERE TO FIND THEM

Elders are everywhere. The first place to look for elders is in your own family. Talking to them will also give you a chance to learn about your own family history.

Ask your friends about older people in their families and visit with them.

There are nursing homes and retirement communities full of elders who want visitors. Talk to them.

TALKING WITH ELDERS

The best way to learn from elders is to listen to them. You can formally interview them, or you can just go visit them and chat.

Just as we have to learn how to talk to kids, we've also got to take time to work out communication with elders. Here are a few tips on how to get the most out of your elder.

- Maintain your sense of humor. The more you can laugh with each other, the more information you'll get and the more fun you'll have.
- Pay attention. We all love to have attention paid to us.
- Be as direct as possible. The clearer you are in what you're asking, the clearer they'll be in their answer.
- Choose a socio-appropriate elder. If you live in a city, consult urban elders for info. An exurban elder might have good advice on how to store a butchered pig but couldn't answer questions about hanging clothes from the fourteenth floor.
- Take notes. Write down the things you think are important and ask for clarification whenever you need it.
- If possible, work alongside your elders. You can learn a lot by watching the way they approach tasks they've done all their lives. What's more, they might have some suggestions for you after seeing the way you work.

TIPS FROM ELDERS

Here's some advice from elders on how to live green, cheap, and happy in the New Depression.

- Use nature to your advantage whenever possible. Read by sunlight. Freeze things on your porch or windowsill.
- Barter. Accept nonconventional payments for your services, such as dinner or a pound of potatoes. Trade things you don't need for things you do.
- Think about what you really need. Don't buy things just because you can afford them. Don't replace things that are still usable.
- Don't buy anything until you can pay for it. Decide

SAMPLE TOPICS FOR TALKING WITH ELDERS

Here are a few areas in which elders might have useful advice
with questions to get you started; fill in others as you go.

1. Electricity
   - How did you keep cool in summer without air
     conditioning?
   - How did you read at night?

   - _____

   - _____

   - _____

2. Running water
   - How much water did you use each day?
   - What did you do with your gray water?

   - _____

   - _____

   - _____

3. Food
   - How did you preserve food?
   - How did you get food?

   - _____

   - _____

   - _____

4. Entertainment
   - What did you do to amuse yourselves?
   - What games did you play?

   - _____

   - _____

   - _____

5. Health
   - How did you take care of your medical needs?
   - Where did you get medicine?

   - _____

   - _____

   - _____

6. Repairing things
   - How did you learn to fix things?
   - What have you fixed?

   - _____

   - _____

   - _____

7. Transportation
   - How often did you get to town?
   - How did you get where you were going?

   - _____

   - _____

   - _____

8. Fitness
   - How did you stay in shape?

   - _____

   - _____

   - _____

   - _____

what you need. Find out how much it will cost. Save your money.

- Live without some things. Don't turn on all the lights when it gets dark. Put on a sweater instead of turning up the heat.
- Repair things. Darn the holes in your socks. Fix your tape deck.
- Don't rush into a project. Think about it from all angles. Figure out the most efficient way to do it.
- Whenever possible, do two things at once to conserve energy. When Warren's family boiled their own maple syrup in the spring, his mother placed a pot of meat and potatoes in the boiling sap. She also boiled eggs right in the sap.
- Do what needs to be done when it needs to be done. Instead of watching TV, sharpen the kitchen knives.
- Never pile green, wet hay in the barn. It could spontaneously combust, and the barn could go up in flames.

Chapter 7:
The K Force

Kids today are radical Earthlings. They're pollution conscious and eco-savvy. They know what animals are in trouble and why. They're Fossil Fuel Foes. The greenhouse effect is part of their science curriculum. Comic strip characters are worried that acid rain will destroy the rain forests *and* their hairdos.

Kids understand their part in the way Earth works. They know about the impact people have had and continue to have on our ecosystems. Most of them are standing by to do whatever they can to help everyone's favorite home planet.

This is good news for Earth. It's been a long time since human beings have thought about the planet in a caring way. Kids know that Earth is in trouble and that we are the ones to save it. What's more, they're not cynical. They believe that their actions can make a difference.

They have to believe this. They're scared. Television and radio bring reality directly to our kids. They get the same information we do. They know there are holes in the ozone layer. They know the world is getting hotter. They know that oil spills happen all the time and really hurt the environment. They know that too many people means many will starve.

These are frightening times for our children—and for us. We are all living with the fear that our planet can be made uninhabitable. This knowledge is transforming childhood. Many kids today are as likely to be thinking about the dangers of global warming as they are to be thinking about sports.

Kids have a lot of power on this planet. When kids get together and take a stand on an issue, grown-ups can't ignore them. Consider:

- When kids learned that Starkist used fishing methods that killed dolphins, they wrote so many letters that Starkist changed their fishing techniques.

- When kids found out that snow leopards in the Himalayas were in big trouble, they wrote to the Minister of Wildlife in India. He was inundated with requests to protect these big cats. He responded by promising to do all he could to save them.

- When ten-year old Melissa Poe learned about pollution, she wrote to President Bush. The letter he sent in reply told her to "just say no" to drugs. Melissa didn't give up. She got a local advertising agency to put her letter on billboards. She appeared on the "Today Show" to ask President Bush to think about Earth. Although Melissa got very little satisfaction from the president, she didn't let his lack of interest discourage her. Instead, she founded her own Earth-activist group—Kids For A Clean Environment. Kids FACE now has over twenty thousand members dedicated to saving the planet.

Children demonstrate time and again that they are eager to help. It's up to us to encourage this and direct their incredible energy. Green, cheap, and happy people are hiring kids because they are an energetic, inexpensive source of labor. As long as you don't pay a child more than fifty dollars in a calendar quarter, you don't have to pay Social Security, and your appointment to the cabinet won't be jeopardized.

There's no reason why kids should not work. The concept of childhood as a carefree garden is a strictly modern invention. Historically, children have been supporting members of the family. Tiny tots helped gather nuts and berries. Teens went on hunts and helped dress the meat.

Most kids will jump at the opportunity to earn some money. They like having a little pocket change or saving up for something they really want. What's more, kids are aware that work is good for them. They believe that it helps make them more responsible and gives them a headstart on life.

> Andrew Sherman for hire! I will do odd Jobs around your house or business
>
> Call ANDREW SHERMAN

ANDREW SHERMAN, ENTREPRENEUR

Twelve-year-old Andrew Sherman has been working ever since he was a little kid. Jobs Andrew has held include waste management (cleaning stalls in a neighbor's barn), consulting, stacking wood, and mowing the grass with a push mower.

"My favorite is mowing the lawn because it's fun with grass going everywhere," he says. "Plus it's good exercise."

Ordinarily, Andrew gets anywhere from $2 to $2.50 an hour. One of his highest paying jobs was as consultant to P3, an eco-magazine for kids. Andrew read every manuscript and gave the editors his comments before a word was sent to the typesetter. For that Andrew received five dollars. During his video game phase, he requested that he be paid entirely in quarters.

In the summer of 1992, Andrew tried advertising. He made a lot of signs offering his services. He handed them out to his friends, who hung them on their refrigerators. The Madison Avenue approach seemed to pay off. He estimates he made between fifty and seventy-five dollars.

"I got quite a few phone calls," said Andrew. "One or two a month, which is kind of a lot for a kid."

Like most kids, Andrew saves some of his money and spends some on impulse buys. Working gives Andrew the freedom to spend money on what he wants.

"Right now I'm putting most of my money into sports,"
he says.

Andrew also realizes that working now will help him out
in the future.

Working gives me discipline and teaches me
responsibility. Like when you're mowing the
lawn, make sure you don't cut the roses in half.
—Andrew Sherman

TWO GOOD REASONS TO HIRE KIDS

1. Kids save you money. Kids will work for less money
than grown-ups because they have fewer opportunities for
getting it. Hiring kids means your cost will be lower.

2. Kids are the future. Working teaches kids skills they
need to survive. It teaches them responsibility and the causal
relationship between doing something and getting something
for it. It encourages them to be independent, and the more
independent we can raise our kids to be, the better it will be
for Earth and the future.

More Reasons to Hire Kids

Grown-ups aren't the only ones who think hiring kids is a good
idea. Kids think it's a good idea, too—especially when the
employer isn't their parents. "We get paid more by other
grown-ups," says eleven-year-old Patrick.

Here are some of the reasons why kids think hiring the
Kid Force is good business.

- Emma: "We learn responsibility." Most kids know that
  working will teach them to be better adults.
- CJ: "Kids have more energy." Kids are aware that they
  are more active and more energetic than grown-ups,
  and they know the value of this commodity.
- August: "It keeps us active and not just sitting around."
- Joey: "If you want to buy a car when you're sixteen, you

won't have enough money if you don't have a job." Kids
learn quickly the value of saving money.
- Morgan: "Kids' backs don't crack when they bend over."
  Kids perceive grown-ups as ancient. They know their
  youth is valuable in working situations.

TOP KID JOBS

Kids are ready and willing to work. There are plenty of jobs
you can hire them to do to save you time and money (or to
help out an elder neighbor or relation) and teach them how
to live on Earth. Here are a few jobs kids want you to hire them
to do:

Planting	Horse care
Bean picking	Lawn mowing
Weeding	Painting
Housecleaning	Leaf raking
Pet care	Doing things for elders
Trash removal	Snow shoveling
Babysitting	Dog walking
Dishwashing	Car washing
Farmwork	

PERSONNEL MANAGEMENT

For the most part, kids are good workers. But problems do
arise. Here are some tips to help you communicate with your
work force in a way that will reduce mistakes and lower frus-
tration levels.
- Be clear. You must think out the steps in advance and
  tell them in an easy-to-remember order.
- Have the kid write down what you say and read it back
  to you. You must be sure you both agree on the task.
- Answer all questions. Kids can think of problems or
  alternatives that might never occur to an adult.
- Check with the parents. You've got to be sure that they
  know what the kid's responsibility is and that they are
  willing to help out if necessary. It's also good to dis-

cuss transportation with parents since they might have to chauffeur your employees to and from work.

- Expect misunderstandings. Grown-ups and kids are different and there are bound to be glitches as you work out your working relationship.
- Quick jobs are better. Kids like to see the end of the job in sight. Who doesn't?

PAYMENT

Minimum wage varies depending on where you live. One thing is certain, though, kids definitely work more cheaply than grown-ups. A good hourly wage is about $2.50. Kids prefer to be paid in cash. Get a receipt from them. Kids love to sign their names and it gives them practice in cursive.

SAMPLE RECEIPT FOR KID FORCE EMPLOYEES

I, _____ ,

have received _____

from _____

for _____ .

That is payment in full.

_____

Signature   Date

TOP TEN THINGS KIDS SAVE UP FOR

Kids like to spend money as well as you do. And they can stay focused on their spending goals. Many kids put as much as fifty percent of everything they make into a savings account.

Here are ten things kids are likely to save for.
1. Clothing
2. A stereo
3. College
4. A car
5. A horse
6. Baseball stuff
7. Camp
8. A trip to DisneyWorld
9. A four-wheeler
10. A bicycle

IN THEIR OWN WORDS
Fifth-graders tell you why they like to work.

"I like to work to earn money because when I get paid I put it in the bank towards college. When I babysit on the weekend I get paid ten dollars for working from 8:00 P.M. to 1:00 A.M. I also work by dusting the house, vacuuming, and doing the dishes."   *—Erin Gray, 11*

"I like to work to get some money. When I don't get money, I try to enjoy working as much as I can. I have fun mowing lawns. I guess it's because I always liked to tear up grass. Sometimes it feels good to help other people by doing chores."   *—Steve Fontaine, 10*

"I like to work a lot because if I save I can go to college and get a car. My favorite kind of work is working with animals and with children. I also like to work because it can be fun and you can see how grown-ups feel."
                                    —Marjolaine Madore, 11

"I like to work because it's a head start on life and you learn about the real world. The money I get I save for important things like a car and college. I think the reason parents

make kids work is to tell them that they have to get a job to
live."   *—Nicole Pothier, 10*

"I like to work for a lot of reasons. I like getting money. I
like doing things to help people. I like knowing that I did something good. I like to get a head start because I'll do it when I'm
older. My young bones can do more things than someone who
is older."   *—Ally Welsh, 10*

"I like to work because it relieves me of some stress. I like
my work because I get dirty and sweaty. My job is piling wood.
I like piling wood because it builds up my muscles. And it gives
me experience in what the real world will be like. I get paid like
a real job."   *—Joey Rawding, 12*

"If we work, it's our money and we earned it so we can't
get in trouble for what we buy."   *—Kim Carr, 13*

Chapter 8:
Join the Earth Gym

Earth is the ultimate workout planet, offering a wide variety of natural ways to stay in shape. Earth has some serious equipment: mountains, pools, cliff faces, scaffolding. And Earth's free weight selection is major: logs, rocks, hay, groceries, and a lot more. In fact, Earth has everything a gym has, except a convenient wall of mirrors.

No one will argue that being fit is important to your health. Studies have consistently shown that a fit body lasts longer and costs less in medical maintenance. Many people are working out harder than ever to keep their bodies in shape. They'll squeeze a fitness routine in before work, at lunch, or after work.

Until recently, workouts were not something that people had to fit into their lives. People's lives *were* their workouts. Every major muscle group was working for survival. Hunters and gatherers walked miles every day to collect the food they needed, so their quads were strong. In agricultural societies, farm labor—lugging water, plowing furrows, hauling wood— provided an intense upper body workout. Even transportation provided some sort of fitness benefit; riding horses develops leg muscles, and driving horses produces massive forearms.

But the more high-tech our lives, the less active. Fewer and fewer humans have the fit life. Most of us have the sit life—we sit all day at a desk taking orders or writing copy or making deals. To stay fit, we go to the gym at lunch or run after work.

Fitness can be costly—both to you and to everyone's favorite home planet. Your out-of-pocket expenses include high gym membership fees and gym fashion that has to be purchased: Lycra, Spandex, CrossTrainers.

In Earth terms, gyms use an incredible amount of energy. The lights are always on. They're either heated or air-conditioned all year long. They require vast amounts of water for showers, drinking fountains, washing machines, toilets, and pools. And the smell of chemical disinfectants and bleach is everywhere.

Green, cheap, and happy people join the Earth Gym and Incorporate an Earth Workout into their days. They're saving money, staying in shape, and keeping Earth in shape, too. The Earth Workout saves energy and water, and builds your biceps, triceps, quadriceps, lats, pecs, and abs. The Earth Gym has no membership fee, it's open twenty-four hours, and every workout is EC (environmentally correct).

WARNING: As with all fitness programs, consult a doctor before you begin.

THE EARTH WORKOUT
All Earth Workouts have five things in common:

1. They strive for minimum Earth-impact. They use little energy except your own. They don't require high-tech machinery or special outfits.

2. They take advantage of the available equipment. Hills, stairs, hay bales, grocery bags, shovels—these are the workout aids of the Earth Gym.

3. They fit into your life. Whether it's taking the stairs or hauling logs, every activity assumes fitness potential.

4. They develop your body in ways useful for life on Earth. When you work out at a gym you come away pumped, but you

have not trained your muscles to do anything practical. How many times in real life will you be called upon to press 240 pounds? But once you get strong enough to carry eighteen logs into the house three times a week, you have developed muscle skills that help you survive.

5. They help you become more independent and self-sufficient. Earth Workouts require you to do things for yourself, rather than relying on a device or service employee to do it for you. This saves money, too, in purchases and tips.

DEB RAVENELLE, EXURBAN EARTH ATHLETE

Deb Ravenelle, thirty-one, is one fit human being. She ought to be. Her daily routine incorporates more fitness activities than the average person would do in one week. No matter what season it is, Deb can be sure that she will lift, stretch, carry, walk, squat, twist, bend, and pull.

A day's work for Deb could be any number of things—logging, sugaring, plowing, planting, and weeding, to name just a few. What she does depends a lot on what season it is.

Each season has its own aerobic value. In winter, Deb can be outdoors eight hours a day walking through the snow, cutting down trees, and using her horses to drag logs out of the woods. In spring, she'll lift and carry seven hundred buckets of sap from the tree to the storage tank once a week for at least a month. In summer, she'll plow her garden with her horses.

"Each season is so different," says Deb. "I really like them all. I wouldn't want to do one thing all year. I like the transition."

Deb does most of her work with horses. In summer and winter, she drives her team of fifteen-hundred-pound Belgians—Champ and King. And in spring, she and her business partners use another team of horses to gather sap for maple syrup.

"I like every aspect of my work when I've got my horses in harness," says Deb.

The horses keep Deb in excellent shape. In the fall, she stacks nearly five hundred bales of hay in her hayloft. Bales can weigh anywhere from twenty-five to forty pounds. Every morning from late fall through late spring, Deb lifts and carries three bales to feed the horses. She carries buckets of water to them at least twice a day.

The harnesses give Deb a terrific upper-body workout. Each harness weighs seventy-five pounds and has to be hoisted up over Deb's head and settled on the broad back of Champ or King. Driving the team requires use of her forearms and shoulders.

Deb has always been very active. She was a long-distance runner in high school. She found school confining and quickly became a fan of the Earth Workout.

"In high school it was like you weren't in a situation where you could be physical. You had to squeeze it into an hour a day," says Deb. "I always thought that was a drag."

Deb always knew she wanted to work outdoors. Since she graduated from college, she's been working out in the Earth Gym. She started at a small farm doing chores and caring for sheep, horses, goats, and cows. She then moved on to a horse farm, where she took care of thirty horses. For a while she worked for a big sugaring concern. They had six teams of horses and twenty thousand taps— all gathered by hand.

"I knew my arms were getting bigger," said Deb.

In 1981 she moved to her own farm and bought her own horses. She plows her garden with them and grows vegetables she sells locally.

Deb rarely gets a day off. On the days she does rest, she really rests.

"When I take a day off in the winter, I don't even want to go outside," says Deb.

BRIAN ATWATER, URBAN EARTH ATHLETE

Brian Atwater doesn't take public transportation to work. He doesn't drive his own car either. Every day, he straps his papers onto his bike rack, puts on his helmet, and pedals through the streets of Seattle to his office at the University of Washington. This Earth Gym member knows his cycling workout well. He knows just which stretches on the four-mile round trip will pump his quads and which stretches he can coast on.

At the office, Brian continues his Earth Gym training workout. He takes the stairs, not the elevator.

"There are only four flights," says Brian. "But it's still more active than riding."

Brian's work as a geologist doesn't confine him to an office on campus. Fitness is built into his field work.

"When I'm out in the field," he says, "I get lots of exercise. It's all outdoor stuff. Sometimes I have to get to my work site by canoe. Then I dig with a shovel all day, a great back workout. I often push core barrels twenty feet into the earth and pull them back up." A core barrel is a device that picks up samples of Earth's strata for analysis.

Brian's fitness level fluctuates. When he has long periods at his desk, he's less fit. When his work involves more time in the field, he's in better shape.

"When you work every day out there you get some kind of workout," he says.

Brian eschews fitness facilities. He prefers the open spaces and freer schedule of the Earth Workout.

I have never belonged to a gym. I've always managed to incorporate exercise into my day either getting to and from work or doing work.

—Brian Atwater

How is the Earth Workout working for him?

"I'm in average shape," Brian says, "for a geologist."

HOW TO BE YOUR OWN TRAINER

The Earth Workout can be strenuous or easy. It's up to you. You are your own trainer in the Earth Gym, and as trainer, you've got to put together the best possible workout. Here are a few things to think about as you create your Earth Workout.

- Consider where you live. Geography plays a big role in the Earth Workout. If you live in the city, your workout will be different from the exurban workout.
- Consider where you work. Some work situations afford employees better opportunities for fitness than others. A street-level insurance office won't have the stair-climbing potential of a ten-story office building.
- Be flexible. The Earth Workout isn't an hour in the gym with fifty other panting, grunting fitness fans. You'll work out when you can. You might walk up five flights of stairs in the morning, then curl fifteen pounds of groceries after work.
- Dress accordingly. What you wear to work is what you work out in. Contrary to popular belief, comfort and style are not mutually exclusive. You can find clothing that will fit in with your work and workout needs.
- Be patient. Depending on what your Earth Workout opportunities are, results may take a long time to see. But eventually your body will begin to look and feel better than ever.

EARTH WORKOUT EXERCISES

Here's a list of individual exercises that can be done at the Earth Gym. Each workout can be made more intense by adding reps. Intensifiers have been added to some.

- Bucket Shoulder Shrugs. With a filled, balanced sap bucket in each hand, do 3 sets of 10 shrugs as you carry the buckets to the storage tank.
- Bucket Obliques. Holding a full water bucket in each hand, lean left and right as you carry the water to your garden. Do 3 sets of 10 each.
- Harness Curl. Grasping the harness in both hands, curl 3 sets of 10 before putting it on the horse's back.
- Hay Bale Clean and Jerk. Hoist one 40-pound bale to your hips, flip it, and toss it. Wear a lower-back support belt and remember to use your thighs.

- Firewood Squats. Squat down. Load your arms with firewood. Stand up. Squat and stand 3 times before taking the wood to the stove.
- Garden Tool Shoulder Lifts. Holding a rake in one hand and a shovel in the other, do 3 sets of 10 lifts on your way to the pumpkin patch.
- Shoveling Abs. Tense your stomach muscles as you shovel. The more work you can do with your abs, the easier it is on your back. And your stomach will flatten nicely.
- Wheelbarrow Hamstring Builder. Push a wheelbarrow full of stones from the garden to the stone pile. Do 3 trips.
- Grocery Bag Upper-Body Workout. Do bicep curls, tricep curls, and shoulder lifts with a full grocery sack.
- Laundry Leg Routine. Hoist your full bag of laundry to your shoulders. Do squats. Carry it downstairs. Jog with it to your laundry. Carry it upstairs.
- The Real Stairmaster. Run up all stairs any time you have to go up. Try stepping over every other step.
- Newspaper Curls. Lift a week's worth of baled newspapers to build your biceps. Do 3 sets of 10 reps on the way to your recycling center.
- Dishrag Forearm Wring. Grasp your dishrag in both hands. Twist it firmly in opposite directions until it's completely wrung out. Wipe your counters. Rinse and repeat.

Earth Gym Equivalency Chart
Here's a chart to help you calculate your free weights.

Earth Gym	Conventional Gym
1 piece of 16-inch firewood	10 lb. dumbbell
1 3-gallon bucket of water	24 lb. dumbbell
1 hay bale	40 lb. dumbbell
2 8-gallon buckets of sap	64 lb. dumbbell

EARTH WORKOUTS ON YOUR HOME TURF
Here are a few ideas for Earth Workouts. Find the one that fits your geographic location. Try it out. Give it a personal spin. When you've got a routine you like that works, write *Earth Gym* on the front of your workout sweatshirt.

The Urban Earth Workout
A really good Earth Workout is harder to find in the city, but it's there.

Walk to work.

Do briefcase curls. Then, holding the briefcase in one hand, flex your wrist to develop your forearms. If the sidewalk is not too crowded, you can even work out your delts with briefcase shoulder lifts.

Whenever possible, use the Real Stairmaster—both up and down. Take stairs two at a time going up for ripped quads.

In the office, don't buzz someone via the intercom. Walk to their office. Walk your own errands. You can put on miles in interoffice movement.

Walk at least five blocks to a restaurant or deli for lunch. Walk back.

After work, do grocery curls for awesome biceps, shoulders, forearms, and triceps.

On weekends, jog around town and look for Earth Gym equipment that will give you a real Earth Workout. Use scaffolding for leg lifts. Don't be afraid to use playground equipment. Monkey bars are great for leg lifts, chin-ups, and dips.

The Suburban Earth Workout
The suburbs can be serious leg builders.

Do your roadwork on the way to your commuter transit. Walk to the station in the morning. Put your execu-wear and files in a backpack and jog home at night.

Push a reel mower for major hams and quads. Raking leaves is a great lat workout. Pruning branches will give you forearms of iron.

Let your shower water run into a three-gallon bucket

while it warms up. Carry the bucket out to the garden to water the flowers. Start by filling it partially and work your way up to full. Do shoulder lifts and try to curl it.

Retire your snowblower and shovel your sidewalks or suburban driveway.

The Exurban Earth Workout

When it comes to incorporating fitness into your daily life, the rural counties have it all over the urban areas.

Chop wood to define the delts. Throw wood to pump up the shoulders. Carry water to carve the biceps and build up the thighs and calves. Shovel dirt and manure for an upper-body workout no Nautilus can match. Drag brush for awesome hams and quads. Do shoulder shrugs with hay bales. Curl the compost pail on your way to the heap.

EARTH WORKOUT FORM

NAME_____

WORKOUT TYPE_____

DATE BEGUN_____

Exercise	# of Reps	Date	Comments, Modifications
_____	_____	_____	_____
_____	_____	_____	_____
_____	_____	_____	_____
_____	_____	_____	_____
_____	_____	_____	_____
_____	_____	_____	_____

COPING WITH SWEAT

Sweat is a natural part of staying fit. Sweat cools you down when you're hot. It's your body temperature regulator.

We've been bombarded with Madison Avenue hype telling us that sweat is terrible. It stinks. It's dirty. It's just not civilized. *Not true.* Sweat is a necessary part of life on Earth. And if you're healthy and eat well, your sweat won't stink too much.

When you fit your workout into your day, you might sweat and have no time to shower. Don't panic! If you really feel strongly about it, you can always give yourself a quick underarm and face wash. (For more about coping with sweat, see Chapter 9.)

DESIGN YOUR OWN EARTH WORKOUT

After a while you'll start to see fitness opportunities everywhere. Crosstraining—moving between urban, suburban, and exurban workouts—is encouraged. Use the form on the opposite page to create an Earth Workout for yourself.

Chapter 9:
Clean Enough

People today have a warped idea of cleanliness. We think dirt is dirty, but we think replacing dirt with chemicals is clean. Chemicals are better, we reason, because they have no germs in them. Germs are what scare us about dirt. And we have Joseph Lister, Scottish physician, to thank for that.

In 1865 Joseph Lister used carbolic acid, a sewer disinfectant, to clean the compound fracture wound of a young boy. The boy's six-week, pus-free recovery convinced Lister that bacteria were the cause of infection. He realized that sterile was the way to go if you wanted live post-op patients.

Prior to Lister's discovery, medicine—and indeed, life itself—was conducted amid a lot of dirt. Too much dirt, in fact. Dirt was found on surgical instruments, on cutlery, on food, in beds, in houses, and on people. Raw sewage ran in the streets. People never bathed. Much of this was due to Christianity. In attempting to remove all bodily temptation from us sinners, the Church looked down on the pleasures of bathing, not to mention nudity. So people wrapped themselves in clothing that they virtually never removed. People got soaked when they were baptized and after that, only in a driving rain. The

Middle Ages were a breeding fest for bacteria. Infections, diseases, putrid odors, and plenty of death were everywhere.

Lister's discovery of germs resulted in today's multi-billion dollar market for germ-terminating products—bathroom cleansers, scouring powder, deodorants, antiperspirants, air fresheners, detergents.

This fear of germs touched off an extreme reaction. We concluded that if eliminating some bacteria in the operating room was good, wiping out germs altogether would be even better. There would be no disease. There would be no foul odors. Death would be forestalled. We boomeranged from the filth of the Middle Ages to the idea that we could somehow create a germ-free world. This is where our thinking took a sharp turn into The Twilight Zone.

We are on a germ rampage, using lethal chemicals to kill bacteria and mask their odors. We pour products down our toilets that say *DANGER. Corrosive. Harmful if swallowed. Protect eyes when handling.* We roll aluminum zirconium trichlorohydrex gly in an antiperspirant base of cyclomethicone and dimethyl benzyl ammonium chloride under our arms to stop a little sweat and body odor.

Our germ fetish is costly—both to us and to Earth. We spend billions of dollars buying products that will make our wash stainless, our glasses spotless, and our bodies odorless. We deplete some of Earth's resources by producing these products and we damage others by washing them into our rivers and oceans. Then we fill our overfull landfills with the discarded containers.

Our houses and offices have never sparkled more. But in keeping germs at bay, we have never stopped to ask ourselves whether the chemicals weren't worse than the germs. Any chemical that kills one life-form can't be that good for anything living. And many of the chemicals in our cleansers and hygiene products poison our environment. Obviously, a single stick of deodorant is not highly toxic, but the cumulative effect of all the toxics in all the products is significant. And unnecessary.

No one wants to return to the Middle Ages. We've learned

that too much dirt is not good. But too little dirt and too many chemicals isn't good either. Happily, there is a middle ground: Clean Enough. The Clean Enough philosophy is based on two simple premises:

1. Dirt is a part of life on Earth.

Billions of tons of space dust land on Earth every day. Crumbs fall on the floor. Knees get grass stains.

2. Odors are a part of life on Earth.

Everything—from death to you to roses—has a distinctive scent. Some are pleasant. Some are unpleasant.

Green, cheap, and happy people are adopting the Clean Enough philosophy. They're spending less on cleansing products, and they're learning to live with some bacteria. They've figured out that replacing dirt and odors with toxic chemicals is not cost-effective for them or the planet.

THE TRUTH ABOUT BACTERIA

Our quest for an odor-free, germ-free life is, of course, totally unrealistic. On Earth, there is no such thing.

Certainly there are bacteria that cause disease. And yes, as bacteria break down organic waste, they release unpleasant odors. Still, the job they do more than compensates for the smell. Bacteria are microscopic powerhouses. They capture nitrogen from the air and put it into ponds and soil so plants and animals can live. Bacteria break down organic waste into compost—the richest, darkest soil around. Bacteria in our intestinal tracts keep us healthy. In other words, bacteria are our friends.

THE WHITENESS MYTH

One of the most harmful tales told by the Madison Avenue storytellers is that whiter than white is the clean standard. It's simply not true. White isn't necessarily the cleanest color around.When cotton is white it's been bleached, and bleach is one of the most toxic products on Earth. If paper is white, it has been bleached. In the bleaching process, dioxins, a toxic by-product, are released into our soil and water.

The cleanest colors around are natural ones—brown papers and beige cottons.

YOU ANIMAL YOU

Humans are, in fact, animals. We breathe. We move around. We have an odor. Up until about the fifth grade, we think this is incredibly cool. Then we hit adolescence and we try as hard as we can to deny it. Our denial is costing us and Earth a lot.

- We use incredible amounts of water to wash ourselves.
- We discard incredible numbers of plastic containers.
- We release incredible amounts of chemicals into the soil, air, and water.
- We spend incredible dollar amounts on products to mask our odors.

Every animal has its own scent. No two animals smell exactly alike. That's part of being an animal. Our digestive processes cause us to smell a certain way. What we eat affects our odor. Accept and embrace your animal status by learning to live with your own scent. Wash with plain soap and water. Go without deodorant. Find out what your scent is. Maybe it isn't terrible. Maybe it's just how you smell.

PORTRAIT OF THE AUTHOR AS CLEAN ENOUGH

I come from a family with a cleaning disorder. It's cross-generational and not gender-specific. Some of us have a more extreme manifestation than others, but no one has escaped it entirely. Family legend tells of Aunt Celia, who used to wake up at 2 A.M. to vacuum, and Grandpa Morris, who wrapped the garbage in brown paper and string before putting it out for collection. Another family narrative describes the time Aunt Sunnie was caught washing the soap dish.

A background like this is hard to escape. Although I do not make the beds of my guests if they wake up to use the bathroom in the night (as is told in a possibly apocryphal story about Aunt Sunnie), when I clean, I can feel the atavistic pull. Sometimes, if I see a piece of lint on the floor after I've swept, I lick the tip of my finger, pick it up, and put it in my pocket.

Before I adopted the Clean Enough philosophy, I was a prisoner of the quest for a germ-free world. I strived for whiter than white and odor-free. I used bleach on my clothes and in my sinks. I sprayed deodorant and antiperspirant under my arms. I sprayed air freshener after I cooked. I showered and washed my hair every day. I had a different sponge for the toilet, bathroom sink, kitchen sink, kitchen counter, and floor.

It wasn't until I made the connection that on Earth life and dirt go hand in hand that I began to relax. I stopped showering every day. I gave up deodorant. My clothes are somewhat dingy. At first I minded. I thought I was dirty. I *was* dirty, and I *did* smell. But not bad. I smelled like myself.

I got used to it. What helped me get to this point was realizing that I am leaving Earth a little cleaner than if I didn't live the Clean Enough way.

The decision to be Clean Enough really made a difference in my cash flow, too. I buy fewer products, and the products I do buy last longer.

I also learned that some dirt is okay. If the countertop doesn't sparkle after I've wiped the flour off with water and peppermint soap, I know that this "dirt" isn't dirty, it's just flour.

Of course, my mother doesn't always think I'm clean enough. But I know I am.

BECOMING CLEAN ENOUGH

Breaking away from a germ fixation can be tough. Society at large hasn't bought into Clean Enough—yet. Here are a few ways to start making your home and body clean enough. They'll save you money, and they'll help save the planet.

- Shower every other day. Once you've gotten used to this, shower every two days.
- Wash your hair every three days. Natural oils are good for your hair and your scalp.
- Open the windows. You'd be surprised how quickly bad smells disappear when you've got some air circulating.

- Use the same cloth to wash your dishes as you do to wipe your counters.
- Vacuum once a month.
- Give up deodorant. Get used to your own scent.
- Wear the same clothes every day for a week. Change your underwear, however.

CLEAN OR DEADLY?

Here is a description of a few of the most popular cleansing agents and what they do to Earth while they're "cleaning" your house and body.

- Bleach. Bleach whitens and brightens your laundry and disinfects your toilet. Bleach also wreaks havoc on the ecosystem. Once you've flushed it down your toilet or washed it down your water pipes, it continues to kill bacteria everywhere it goes. Harmless, beneficial bacteria die along with the harmful bacteria. What's more, bleach reacts with some other household cleansers to form chlorine gas, which can be lethal.

- Air fresheners. Air fresheners are silly. They trade sterile, chemical odors for the other odors in your home. They are also future garbage. You use them, and then you throw them away.

   Many air fresheners come in aerosol containers. These containers release chemicals that destroy the ozone layer. The ozone layer floats between us and the sun, protecting us from cancer-causing ultraviolet rays. Aerosols and refrigerants and Styrofoam have ripped the fabric of our ozone layer. UV rays are coming in at unprecedented rates. What's more, aerosol containers cannot be recycled and thus become garbage.

   Air fresheners that plug into outlets waste energy in addition to adding chemicals to the air.

- Deodorants. Deodorants deodorize by wiping out the bacteria that live on sweat. They work just like pesticides do. Deodorants don't differentiate between harmful bacteria and the beneficial bacteria that live on and protect the skin from irritation. Deodorants destroy the natural bacterial balance on your skin.

- Antiperspirants. Antiperspirants use chemicals to suppress sweat. Sweat is our internal temperature control mechanism. When we prevent our bodies from sweating, we're preventing our thermostats from regulating our temperatures as necessary.
- Detergent. Detergents are synthetic cleansers. They are poisonous. Many contain phosphates and petroleum products. Some contain chlorine, artificial dyes, and perfumes. They were invented during World War II when the vegetable oils and animal fats used to make soap became scarce. When detergents wash down our drains, the phosphates in them are fuel for algal growth. Algae blooms—too much algae in a body of water—deprive the water of oxygen. This kills off aquatic life that needs oxygen. Dishwashing detergents may leave a residue on your dishes. Those poisons are there every time you put a fork in your mouth.

Green and Cheap Alternatives
Use these products to replace the chemicals.

- Baking soda. Baking soda is one of the most effective household cleansers. And it's biodegradable and safe. Sprinkle some in your sink before you go to bed. When you wipe the sink in the morning, it will be clean. Sprinkle some on cooked-on food and let it stand. The food will come off. Leave an open box in your fridge to remove odors. Baking soda is even good for brushing your teeth.
- Vinegar. Vinegar is a great all-around cleaner. Pour some on a piece of newspaper to clean your windows and mirrors. Vinegar will also remove lime stains from your toilet, your washing machine, and your tea kettle.
- Soap and warm water. Soap is a natural cleanser. Given oxygen and sunlight, soap will break down into a natural, nonpolluting sludge. Soap and warm water will

take out almost any kind of dirt. The important factor is not quantity, it's agitation. If you wash something vigorously, soap and warm water will work. Make your own pollution-free dishwashing detergent by grating a bar of real soap and dissolving it with some baking soda in one-half quart of boiling water. It will be effective for all kinds of dishes and for handwashables as well.

- Furniture polish. Mix two parts olive or vegetable oil with one part lemon juice for a furniture polish that really works.

DIFFERENTIATING DIRT

There are different kinds of dirt on Earth. Some dirt is really dirty. Some is not. Different kinds of dirt require different cleaning techniques. Remember these tips before you attack with the strongest chemical dirt-eradicator around.

- Assess the kind of dirt you're going after and choose the right cleanser for the right job.

    Is it toxic, such as battery acid or windshield wiper fluid? Is it germy, like manure or raw chicken blood? Is it benign, such as flour or bread crumbs? You don't need a disinfectant for flour. Just use soap and water and some elbow grease.
- Wash some dishes without detergent.

    There's no need to wash a cup that held herbal tea with soap at all.
- When you use a toxic cleanser, use it sparingly.

    Once in a while you might have to disinfect the toilet. Go ahead.

FOR WOMEN ONLY

Feminine hygiene is a large part of the hygiene market. Women are exhorted not to give off any female smells whatsoever, particularly during their periods.

Disposable sanitary products were invented so we could get away from our scent. Sanitary napkins and tampons may look and smell good, but they're far from good for us or for Earth.

Tampons and napkins are bleached with chlorine and contain dioxin. Bleach is an irritant. Dioxin is toxic. Why would we want to put these against our skin or inside our bodies?

When we throw them away or flush them down the toilet, we transfer those toxics directly to the earth.

Green, cheap, and happy women are making their own sanitary napkins. These womanpads may not be as convenient or as comfortable as disposable napkins, but they produce a fraction of the garbage and cost a fraction of commercial products.

How to Make Your Own Womanpads

You need four cotton diapers, a pair of scissors, two safety pins, and a roll of cotton.

1. Cut the diapers in half.
2. Fold the halves in half.
3. Place a piece of cotton at one end.
4. Fold the diaper over the cotton and continue folding in three-inch segments.
5. Pin the pad into your underwear.

Womanpad Cleanliness Tips

- Keep a bucket of water with peppermint soap in your bathtub. Throw the dirty pads in there.
- Use the cotton twice, then discard.
- Wash the pads.
- Use the water you've soaked the pads in to water your garden. It's nutrient-rich.

Afterword

I've never been in better shape in my life.

—*Deb Ravenelle*

I personally wash my bod on an average of once every five to seven days, and I've yet to have any complaints from anyone, including my girlfriend and my mother!

—*Rolfe Barron*

These are actual quotes from real people living the green, cheap, and happy lifestyle. People everywhere are finding that in terms of satisfaction, contentment, great bods, and a sense of inner peace, the GC&H way can't be beat.

We hope this book helps you make the GC&H switch. Once you do, you'll be coming up with pithy sayings, too.

Write them here.

_____

_____

_____